THE LAST OF THE
WILD
HORSES

THE LAST OF THE WILD HORSES

Text by MARTIN HARBURY
Photographs by RON WATTS
Preface by RICHARD ADAMS

KEY·PORTER·BOOKS

Half-title: A horse in search of water plants in the Camargue region of
southern France.
Frontispiece: Wild horses gallop along a deserted beach on Canada's
Sable Island.
Page 6: The fierce Przewalski horse of eastern Asia.
Pages 12–13: Horses run through a shallow pond in the Camargue.

Canadian Cataloguing in Publication Data
Harbury, Martin, 1945–
   The last of the wild horses

ISBN 0-919493-35-1 (bound) ISBN 1-55013-642-9 (pbk.)

1. Wild horses. I. Watts, Ron. II. Title.

SF360.H37 1984   599.72′5   C84-098593-2

Key Porter Books
70 The Esplanade
Toronto, Ontario
Canada M5E 1R2

Design by Don Fernley

Printed in Spain

94 95 96 97 98 6 5 4 3 2 1

CONTENTS

PREFACE

*T*here is no other creature which has so deeply affected Man's imagination, entered his soul and captured his heart as the horse. This is not only because for thousands of years nearly all civilised societies have been dependent on the horse. The phenomenon goes far deeper than mere utility.

> Four things greater than all things are, —
> Women and Horses and Power and War.

Kipling's Khyber tribesman, of course, was speaking of horses (and to some extent also of women) primarily as valuable property and status symbols. To him (as to others) it was natural to feel almost as much gratified by possessing a beautiful horse as by being the lover of a beautiful woman. But in speaking of horses and women in the same breath he was expressing his awareness of that ineffable fascination, sublimity and wonder which, time out of mind, have imparted to certain spheres of life values transcending those of mere usefulness, (one might also instance e.g. music, which strictly

7

speaking is of no *use* at all) and on the invisible wings of which the soul is carried towards the divine.

"The head of the celestial horse is the dawn," says the Brihad-aranyaka Upanishad, (a Hindu religious treatise dating from about the 8th century B.C.,) "its eye the sun, its breath the air, its open mouth a fire . . . Its back is heaven, its belly the sky . . . its feet the days and nights, its bones the stars and its flesh the clouds . . . Its yawning is lightning, its shaking the body is thunder, its urinating is rain and its neighing is Voice." Here Creation itself is conceived of as a Cosmic Horse.

Ten thousand years and more before this hymn of praise was first uttered, Palaeolithic Man had expressed on the cave walls of Lascaux the same idea — that of a creature upon which had been conferred something of divinity more than mere human reason could comprehend: a kind of translation into flesh and blood of the harmony sounding eternally in the ears of the gods.

The ancient Greeks, as we all know, worshipped numerous gods and goddesses. Any feature of life which seemed to them too marvellous and inexplicable to be accounted for as a discovery or achievement of mere unaided human ingenuity could only be, in their eyes, a divine gift. Thus, sexual love was the gift of Aphrodite, wine the gift of Dionysos and the smelting and forging of metal the gift of Hephaistos. To the god Poseidon they attributed two mighty and magical benefactions — the ship and the horse.

Gulliver's Travels is perhaps the most misanthropic book ever to gain acknowledgement as a great work of literature. Jonathan Swift felt revulsion for Man in almost every aspect; and that sense of contempt and disgust informs the whole book. Yet if it had been a work solely of disillusionment and odium it would not have endured these 260 years. Swift felt impelled also to express, in Gulliver's last voyage, his notion of an ideal society. Yet even in fantasy he could not bring himself to make it a human society. What creatures could most plausibly be put forward as his ideal beings? He chose Horses. The Houyhnhnms are horses; and their name is a phonetic rendering of a horse's neigh. George Orwell suggested that the reason for Swift's choice was that the horse's ordure is not offensive to man. This is certainly something which would weigh with Swift; but it is, I think, clear that there was more to it than that.

"Friendship and benevolence are the two principal virtues among the Houyhnhnms, and these not confined to particular objects, but universal to the whole race, for a stranger from the remotest part is equally treated with the nearest neighbour, and wherever he goes looks upon himself as at home. They preserve decency and civility in the highest degrees, but are altogether ignorant of ceremony. They have no fondness for their colts or foals, but the care they take in educating them proceeds entirely from the dictates of reason, and I observed my master to show the same affection to his neighbour's issue that he had for his own. They will have it that Nature teaches them to love the whole species, and it is reason only that makes a distinction of persons where there is a superior degree of virtue."

Yet with all respect to Swift, Man's involvement with the horse goes far beyond the level of reason — even 18th century Reason — and beyond the level of the conscious mind.

"Sometimes," says Sir James Frazer in *The Golden Bough*, "the Corn-spirit appears in the shape of a horse or mare. Between Kalw and Stuttgart, when the corn bends before the wind, they say 'There runs the Horse.' At Bohlingen, near Radolfzell in Baden, the last sheaf of oats is called the Oats-stallion. In Hertfordshire, at the end of the reaping, there is or used to be observed a ceremony called 'crying the Mare.' The last blades of corn left standing on the field are tied together and called the Mare. The reapers stand at a distance and throw their sickles at it. After it is cut the reapers cry 'I have her!' Others answer 'What have you?' — 'A Mare! A Mare!' 'Whose is she?' 'A. B.'s,' naming the owner. 'Where will you send her?' 'To C. D.,' naming some neighbour who has not reaped all his corn. In this custom the corn-spirit in the form of a mare is passed on from a farm where the corn is all cut to another farm where it is still standing.

"In the neighbourhood of Lille, when a harvester grows weary at his work, it is said, 'He has the fatigue of the Horse.' The first sheaf, called the 'Cross of the Horse', is placed on a cross of boxwood in the barn, and the youngest horse on the farm must tread on it. The reapers dance round the last blades of corn, crying, 'See the remains of the Horse!' The sheaf made of these last blades is given to the youngest horse of the parish to eat. This youngest horse represents the corn-spirit of the following year, the Corn-foal, which absorbs the spirit of the old Corn-horse by eating the last corn cut."

Not only through folk-lore, but through our dreams, also, the horse runs; and in this mysterious world, over which we have no conscious control, he more often than not appears as a wild horse — no tamed, obedient beast of burden. In this rôle he is one of the great archetypes of the Unconscious. Jung, in *Man & His Symbols*, recounts a dream told him by a middle-aged company director who lived alone, working hard and repressing almost all pleasure and spontaneity.

"I dreamt I owned a big house. In the cellars I found a maze of rooms of which I knew nothing. When I came up from searching them, a smiling, genial man approached me and reminded me that we had been friends when we were boys at school. We walked together through streets to an open, green place, and here three horses galloped past. I knew that they were wild horses, yet they were well-groomed and very beautiful. I said, 'I believe they've run away from military service.' "

The underground maze, says Jung, represents the dreamer's unconscious—those depths of his psyche which he has neglected and of which he knows so little. The old school-friend personifies his spontaneous, carefree childhood, long lost. When the dreamer associates with the friend, the horses break loose from the conscious discipline characterizing his waking life. In this old friend, and in the horses, are symbolized the positive, instinctive powers lost to the dreamer in his waking life.

Another eminent psychiatrist, H. G. Baynes, (writing in the nineteen-thirties) tells a true story of two farm-labourers in East Anglia who were sheltering from a thunderstorm when a clap of thunder burst overhead. "Did ye see the black horse in the sky?" broke out one to the other. "Here," comments Baynes, "we see the mythological moment and the true mythological response. The uneducated peasant has not acquired the habit of responding to life from his higher cortical centres. Instinctively, therefore, he falls back upon the primordial image, with the result that he is still able to respond adequately to a primordial situation. Observe that it is not the thunder as such, but rather the overwhelmingness, the impressiveness of the total experience which brings up the image of the black horse from the archaic depths."

I have said enough to show how inseparably the horse has for countless ages been involved in Man's life on earth; not merely in his practical, utilitarian life, but even more deeply in his imaginative, his metaphysical and his unconscious life. To anyone who appreciates the significance of this, the vital importance of conserving and as far as possible increasing the world's remaining wild horses needs no emphasis.

I quote without comment a passage written about 350 B.C. by a Chinese named Chuang Tzu, (translated by Herbert Giles).

"Horses have hoofs to carry them over frost and snow; hair, to protect them from wind and cold. They eat grass and drink water, and fling up their heels over the champaign. Such is the real nature of horses.

One day Poh Loh appeared, saying, 'I understand the management of horses.'

So he branded them, and clipped them, and pared their hoofs, and put halters on them, tying up their heads and shackling their feet, and keeping them in stables, with the result that two or three in every ten died.

The potter says, 'I can do what I want with clay. If I want it round, I use compasses; if rectangular, a square.'

The carpenter says, 'I can do what I will with wood. If I want it curved, I use an arc; if straight, a line.'

But on what grounds can we think that the natures of clay and wood *desire* this application of compasses and square, of arc and line? Nevertheless, every age extols Poh Loh for his skill in managing horses, and potters and carpenters for their skill with clay and wood.''

For our own sakes we all need to feel and understand the value to the world of the wild horses, those paragons of natural power, grace and beauty. I will go further: we cannot afford to do without them. Anyone who reads this book will, I feel sure, become convinced that that is nothing more than the plain truth.

RICHARD ADAMS

INTRODUCTION

Not so very long ago, wild horses ran free throughout the world. Now, banished by civilization to a few remote and desolate outposts, they make a final stand against the continuing incursions of so-called progress. Their days, like their ranks, are plainly numbered. If nothing changes, they may be in danger of vanishing forever.

Why should this be so? For thousands of years, the horse offered mankind attainment of the most distant horizons; provided food, clothing and weapons; inspired countless artists; enriched our myths and legends. Today, its role in the western world is trivial or anachronistic, confined to pleasure and occasional pageantry. We keep horses to ride, race or bet on; to recall the time when empires toppled with a cavalry charge. The savage riders who swept out of Asia rendered battle itself a nomadic pursuit, changing forever the course of human history. Indeed, the histories of horse and man are irrevocably intertwined. In peace and war, so many of our explorations and achievements were made possible by virtue of mounting a horse — a powerful leap that Jacob Bronowski, in *The Ascent of Man*, correctly terms "a more than human gesture, the symbolic act of dominance over the total creation."

But even the noblest beast of burden fails to inspire in us the same, almost universal fascination as does the image of a wild stallion. Sadly, that stallion is the stuff of dreams, not scientific fact. The *truly* wild horse (apart from the primitive Przewalski, some 400 of which exist in captivity) is possibly extinct. All the beautiful animals we think of as wild horses — the North American mustangs; the horses of Canada's Sable Island; the European Tarpans; the ponies of Britain, Iceland and Scandinavia; the Australian Brumbies; and the all-white marsh horses of the French Camargue — are more properly termed "feral."

This means simply that their domestic ancestors escaped the bonds of civilization and became wild. This designation is important to biologists — feral and wild populations may differ radically in appearance and genetic makeup. However, true wildness captures the public imagination far more than being merely feral and perhaps the image of the world's free-roaming horses has suffered in consequence. Indeed, my five years of in-depth research, consultation with numerous authorities worldwide, and examination of all documentary evidence available to date suggest that these horses are, for all intents and purposes, wild. Having established their ability to survive and reproduce, they quickly relearn or remember the behavior patterns honed to perfection by their distant forebears. But still the feral tag persists. In the worst analysis, such horses are looked upon as little better than vermin, devoid of economic value, occupying land that might be put to better use. The treatment accorded them may vary from country to country — but, in the main, society's most enlightened position is one of benign neglect. If they are wild, after all, they ought to be able to fend for themselves.

We can no longer afford that lofty point of view. For centuries, we have exhibited a profoundly ambivalent attitude toward the horse — envying its freedom while seeking to harness its power, admiring its passion for survival while methodically sealing its fate. This attitude, as we shall see, remains in force today. But today, more than ever before, wild horses require our assistance. We have rendered it impossible for them to live in splendid isolation, maintaining a romanticized and somehow independent existence far apart. They have become, through our deprivations, our responsibility.

1
ORIGINS

*B*etween fifty and seventy million years ago, a brand-new mammal made its debut on the evolutionary stage. Probably camouflaged by a dappled, short-haired coat, it stood only twelve to fifteen inches high, and moved with a fox-like gait on multiple toes through the dense and steaming jungles, browsing on leaves and shrubs.

The North American scientists who discovered this creature's fossilized remains called it eohippus, or "dawn horse." Its appearance marks the beginnings of the long and complex evolutionary trail of the family Equidae. The exact details of this evolutionary history, spanning millions of years, are still subject to scientific debate and ongoing investigation by paleontologists.

We do know that as the earth turned colder, many animals perished, unable to overcome the loss of their jungle habitat. But eohippus was well equipped to deal with the changes—a quality shared by its descendants. Two equally successful branches of the family tree appeared at about this point, one developing into what is now the

17

tapir, the second, into what is now the rhinoceros. In time, several evolutionary blind alleys would also diverge, producing genera that, for many reasons, are no longer living.

Some twenty-two million years later, eohippus had evolved into a larger though not necessarily faster or more agile animal called *Mesohippus*, standing on three toes, perhaps eighteen inches high at the shoulder, or withers (our standard point of height measurement for equids). Most of the growth had taken place in the lower leg. Another development, perhaps made necessary by the first, was a gradual lengthening of the neck. As a result of climatic and geographical changes, equids now lived in a plains environment. *Mesohippus* probably grazed rather than browsed, unlike its predecessors. It also began to develop a specialized set of teeth. Those at the front were able to crop the tougher vegetation, while those at the back chewed and ground it fine.

An artist's impression of *Hyracotherium* reveals the comparatively short legs and neck and the doglike gait of this early creature.
Its appearance gives little hint of later evolutionary developments.

The next sixteen million years produced several further genera including one known as *Merychippus*. It had gained another twenty inches or so, standing about thirty-nine inches at the withers, with a proportional growth in the head and neck. Although it still had three toes like *Mesohippus*, the structure of its feet suggests that it had a distinctive running style. Instead of taking its weight, tapir-like, on a fleshy pad behind its toes, *Merychippus* ran on the enlarged nail of each foot's middle toe—the developing hoof. The two remaining outside toes had meanwhile become shorter, smaller and relatively useless, while the fleshy pad had started to disappear. That process is almost complete in our modern horse, although the pad's last vestige (the ergot, a small growth on the back of the fetlock) remains barely visible.

After another eleven million years—and several more offshoots that would eventually dead-end—the animal, now called *Pliohippus*,

Merychippus, the third stage of evolutionary development, shows radical changes, including increased body size and dramatically longer legs and neck. Note the developing hoof.

had gained another nine inches in height, lost all outer traces of its multiple toes, and further developed a hoof. This animal was probably the direct ancestor not only of today's horse, but of the ass and zebra families. With its identification, we near the end of the trail. Indeed, *Pliohippus* looks disconcertingly familiar. We might also mistake it for a donkey or burro — or for certain wild horses that at this very moment walk the earth.

The evolutionary history of the family Equidae leaves many questions unanswered with regard to the origins of the modern horse, *Equus*. The fossil remains of primitive horses have been located almost everywhere in the world, and paleontologists have identified more than twenty species and subspecies, some of which display great differences — differences that persist in horses today. The many breeds of modern horses are, on close examination, quite unlike. What accounted for the extreme variations in size, appearance, coloration and temperament? And where in the world did the modern horse *Equus* come from?

It will come as a surprise to many people who believe that Spanish conquerors "introduced" the horse to the Americas that conclusive evidence reveals a purely American genesis for equids. This is where the earliest and most complete remains have been unearthed. It was from this starting point that members of the equid family began their long journeys across the globe.

Those journeys took place more than once. In fact, eohippus was first identified from fossils discovered in the south of England, where scientists called it *Hyracotherium*, after the hyrax, an even smaller browsing mammal. But how did the equid family cross what is now the Atlantic Ocean? The riddle is solved when we realize that North America, Europe and Asia were connected, during certain geological periods, by a number of "land bridges" formed by movement of the continents and by the retreating waters of various ice ages. These long-gone highways offered free passage to anything that wanted to migrate and the primitive equids, as noted, were well equipped to cover long distances.

From the first, the equids were distinguished by their mobility. When they moved from forests onto the plains, they could no longer hide from their natural predators — but they could, and did, run. During this period, evolutionary changes included a dramatic increase in the size of the head and the nasal passages and the formation of a larger, stronger neck, as well as a vastly increased lung

capacity. Ever so slowly, over millions of years, the horse was inexorably shaped by nature to fulfill its fleet-footed destiny.

In time, *Equus* became one of the world's foremost travellers,
embarking on a series of wanderings that exposed it to an ever-
widening series of evolutionary variables. Wherever it went — to
Europe, Africa or Asia — it quickly adapted to local conditions.
Back at home, in North America, we may speculate that some
horses crossed into Asia, became subtly altered by a different climate and alien crops, and then returned to breed with the cousins
they'd left behind, adding, in the process, new and confusing spice
to the evolutionary stew.

The causes of these evolutionary changes are open to speculation,
but one thing is certain. A prime factor in the extinction of the
horse in North America was man. The land bridge that enabled
horses to reach the Orient brought the first human beings from the
opposite direction, armed not only with spears and stone knives,
but with other, more deadly "weapons" — exotic diseases, to which
the horse had no immunity.

Before the coming of man, the horse had successfully outdis-
tanced its predators, leaving natural enemies literally behind. But
the combination of germ-laden hunters, rapid climatic change and
frequent natural cataclysms proved too great. The La Brea Tar Pits
in Los Angeles and a bone-strewn watering hole near Orchard,
Nebraska, offer eloquent testimony to the horse's fate in the land of
its birth. (This mid-west location reveals the remains of animals
that appear to have been asphyxiated by a giant dust-cloud.) After a
history of survival and adaptation totalling some sixty million
years, the horse died out in North America between eight and ten
thousand years ago.

Elsewhere, of course, it managed to endure, although often in
constant peril. Early men the world over hunted the horse. Its flesh
became the mainstay of prehistoric diets; its hide provided skins to
warm the cave-dwellers; its bones were fashioned into tools and
armaments. In central France there is a long, narrow outcrop called
the Rock of Solutré, framed by steep cliffs on three sides. At its foot,
scientists have discovered the bones of countless horses, stampeded
over the edge by primitive hunting tribes thousands of years ago.
But even though European and Asiatic horses died by the tens,
perhaps hundreds of thousands, only in North America was the
extermination of the horse complete.

Exactly when and where the horse was first tamed remains
unknown. One radical theory suggests that domestication occurred

some thirty thousand years ago, in which event Cro-Magnon Man was far brighter than he is popularly assumed to have been. Other, more conservative estimates range between five and eight thousand years ago, either in the Middle East or on the Asian steppes.

No one can be certain but, once again, we can to a degree hypothesize. In all probability, the animals most likely to be captured would have been lame or pregnant mares. The latter would have been allowed to wean their offspring, while the owners, nomadic herdsmen accustomed to milking other animals, simply included the horse in their dairy stock. Foals would have become an evening meal, leaving the diners to wrestle with the problem of getting the mare in foal again. This would have been achieved, when she came into heat, by staking her out to attract a passing stallion.

How long before the herdsmen began to play some active, purposeful role in the choice of breeding partners? They would have noticed that certain mares produced stronger offspring than others; that certain stallions, glimpsed on their nocturnal rounds, seemed to sire healthier colts. That conscious decision, lost in the mists of history, marked the end of a truly "natural" selection; and, by some definition, an end to the horse's truly wild state.

How long, then, before someone, in the straggling progress from one camp to another, put the first horse to work, strapping his burden atop its back? How long before a child assumed that place of honor, becoming the first member of a mounted society? How long before a simple travois — two poles resting across the horse's back and dragging on the ground behind — was loaded with a herdsman's worldly goods?

Soon, adults would have coveted the infant's perch, and the tribe would have taken to horseback, one and all. Bridles, reins, saddles and stirrups cannot have been far behind. Now the tribe could greatly extend its grazing grounds, bringing it into contact with neighboring groups who had followed the same course or, at the least, other bands of horses, marginally different from those it had begun with. By this time, the tribesmen, far from eyeing foals with a view to that night's supper, would have kept them until they reached maturity and usefulness. Some colts, of course, would have grown into stallions, offering fresh scope to the first breeding programs. Slowly, inevitably, "man-made" strains or types of horses spread throughout the vast expanses of Eurasia, cross-pollinating and changing with successive generations.

These nomadic peoples kept no records of their activities, no studbook for our inspection. We know nothing of the way they viewed their newly acquired servants, nor if they dimly grasped how totally their halting experiments would affect their lives. Strangely enough, we know more about how far earlier, more primitive men perceived the horse. Deep in the caves of southern France and northern Spain, they left a priceless legacy, hidden for centuries in the hollow darkness.

Today, visitors who gain access to these gloomy caverns must creep through winding passages and past sharp-edged stalactites, enduring the eerie rustle of bats and the constant, oppressive sound of dripping water. Then, when least expected, the guide's flashlight reveals an amazing panorama of sophisticated art, visible on every surface of an underground gallery. Its engraving, design and colorations seem almost modern, recalling Picasso's extreme purity of line. And yet these paintings were executed between ten and twenty thousand years ago, by men who edged along these same tortuous routes, seeking out the most secluded places to record the denizens of a world above.

Why would they go to such pains? One explanation is that primitive man depicted the animals that threatened him in an attempt to defuse their capacity to inspire terror. Perhaps youthful hunters were brought here to undergo initiation rites, suddenly confronted with the very beast that would kill them if it could. Perhaps, in some mystical way, the cavemen sought to absorb the power and essence of their prey by capturing its image. If so, it is natural that the horse, a prime object of their hunts, should be depicted many times; it appears in forty percent of all the paintings.

One aspect strikes the onlooker as peculiar. While other animals are commonly shown pierced by arrows, or surrounded by groups of stick figures, most of the horses are not. Rather, they seem to float unconfined on walls and ceilings, rendered with an almost tangible reverence, as if their hunters, even though they would ascend and seek to butcher them in the morning light, somehow recognized in these particular beings a pure and finally unapproachable beauty.

A modern Przewalski stallion displays his powerful profile and primitive markings. Note the bristling black mane connected with the tail by a dark dorsal stripe.

Right: A painting from Lascaux cave in southern France portrays a horse with some characteristics of the Przewalski, including general coloring, pale belly, vertical black mane, and markings on the now-faded muzzle. Unlike most cave paintings of horses, this one depicts arrow-like objects near the horse.

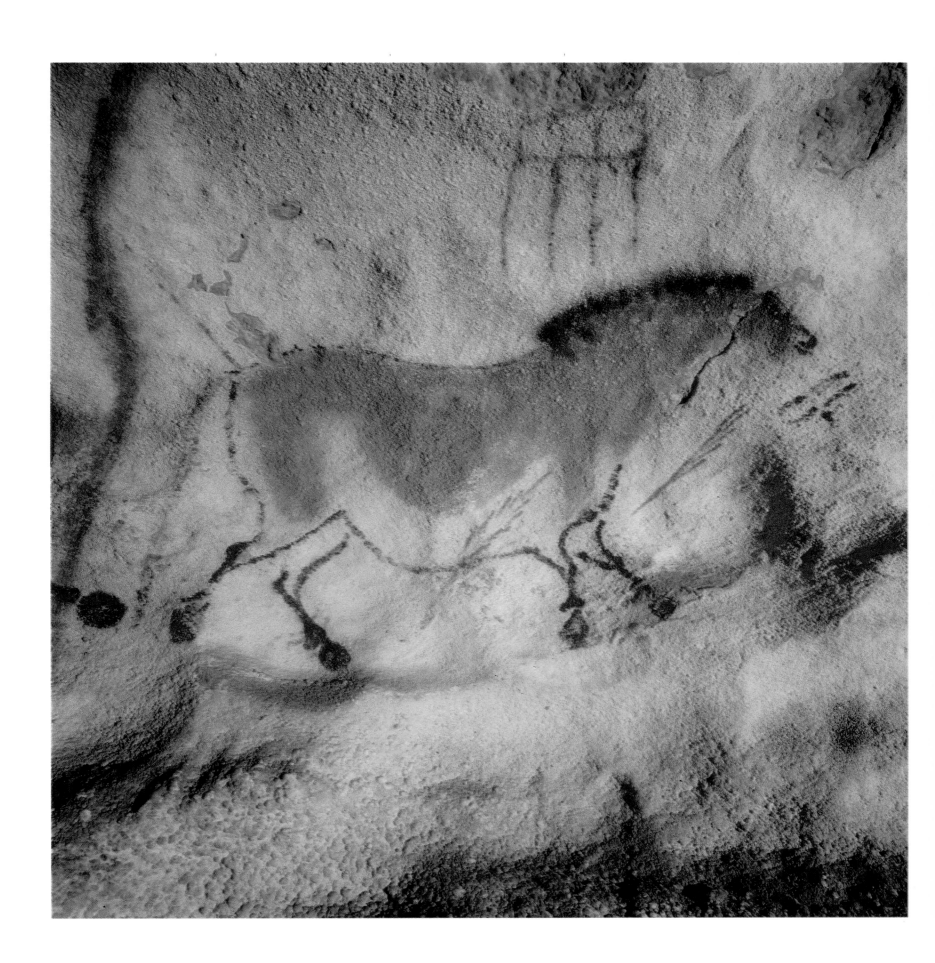

A bedraggled Exmoor pony with its winter coat. Like the Przewalski, it has a stocky build and pale markings at muzzle, eye and belly.

Right: This alert Przewalski shows the beginnings of its shaggy winter coat, a characteristic of all primitive horses.

Feral horses often regain some characteristics of their wild forebears. Both mustangs display a dark dorsal stripe and the foal's legs show faint fingermarks.

Sable Island horses instinctively flee
when surprised.

2
BEHAVIOR

*I*n the open paddock of a country zoo, a group of compact, shaggy horses lower their heads to graze. Their short, bristle-like manes stick straight out as they crop the tufts of grass. Suddenly, a rabid barking from behind a hedge at the paddock's opposite end disturbs the silence. The horses stiffen, rotating their ears, straining to pinpoint its source.

Through the hedge slip two large, cadaverous and wild-eyed dogs. Moving stealthily, though driven by hunger—it has been days since their last full meal — they spy a foal, huddling close to its dam. Wary yet confident, the dogs turn toward it in a menacing pincer movement.

The horses have lived in captivity all their lives, as did the majority of their immediate ancestors. But now, faced with a danger they've never encountered before, they react instantly and instinctively. Squealing and snorting, they form a circle around the foal. The dogs close in, with a slinking, belly-to-the-ground rush. The horses wait, skittish but somehow prepared.

31

The first dog, braver or hungrier than its companion, leads the attack. Sensing an easy kill, he expects the horses to panic and run. Almost on top of one pregnant mare, the weak link in a moving barrier, he poises himself to spring, a growl rising in his throat. As the mare and her neighbors shift from side to side, the dog makes out his opening. He launches himself at his quarry, but the horses don't react as he'd planned. The gap closes, as two pairs of hooves come out of nowhere, flashing and lethal. Only one hoof lands, catching him a glancing blow that nevertheless bowls him over backwards. Yelping in pain, he beats a hasty retreat, covered by his less impetuous hunting partner. The dog, if only he knew it, is lucky to escape. Had he been alone, momentarily stunned by the impact, he would have been trampled to death in seconds.

Calm returns to the meadow and the horses resume their browsing — forgetting, until the next time they are required, their far-off Mongolian roots. Only the stallion is slower to relax, as he stands between the mares and the disappearing threat, sniffing the air and stamping out his final defiance.

In a few moments, we have witnessed the extraordinary transition of these Przewalski horses from placid, well-fed inhabitants of a guarded zoo to a cunning, self-sufficient and highly dangerous band of wild animals. At the first sign of unfamiliar danger, they reverted totally and with incredible speed, reacting exactly as would have their forebears and wild cousins. But how did they know to form, as a group, what was in fact the most effective defensive position? Why didn't they take flight — the horse's first line of defence since the dawn of time — abandoning the foal to be protected only by the stallion? The answers lie in the nature of the horse's social structure, and the high degree of communication that exists among members of a particular group.

The behavior patterns of horses the world over are both subtle and complex. Horses are among the most social of animals, and their activities are extremely formal and ritualized, especially in a wild state (although the Przewalskis' response shows just how fine a line exists between so-called domesticity and wildness).

The natural structure of a band of horses is the family group. As with families everywhere, there is a head of the household — the stallion — who leads the pecking order. A mature stallion gathers about him a harem of mares, with which he breeds. Very few stallions, however, are satisfied with a single mare, and much of a stallion's waking hours are spent in concerted efforts to acquire more. The first mare he selects is generally the dominant, or lead mare, and ranks just below him in familial authority, followed at a distance by second-string mares, subordinate stallions and numerous offspring.

Everything that occurs within a harem or family group appears to be governed by a strict and (with minor variations) universally accepted set of rules — an equine code of good conduct. Eating, drinking and movements of the group, bathing, grooming and breeding all take place with the utmost order and decorum. Transgressions, on the other hand, are met with a progressively more severe system of warnings and punishments.

The harem is a strongly patriarchal unit in which the stallion serves as final arbiter of every action and interaction. When a harem moves, the lead mare takes up a position in front, and chooses the route. The stallion takes his post in the rear, between his family and immediate or potential danger. This strategic placement allows him both to fight a rearguard action, if necessary, and to command the movements of the horses under his control. Stallions take their responsibilities very seriously, and have been known to pick up and half-drag, half-carry very young foals between their teeth in the course of a high-speed chase.

This "driving" attitude also surfaces when a mare strays away from the group. Its intensity reveals much about the stallion's frame of mind. Head lowered, he stretches his neck and weaves it snake-like from side to side, directing an errant wanderer back to the fold. The lower his head, the worse his mood, and the more likely he will be to enforce the lesson with a nip of his powerful teeth. Few subordinate horses dare to ignore the warnings of a testy stallion — and then, not for long.

Horses are constantly on the move, but the reasons behind their migrations are somewhat obscure. Previous generations travelled out of sheer necessity, because their grazing lands were overcrowded. Dominant stallions and their harems made life so uncomfortable for subordinate animals that they sought their own, less populated stamping grounds. Perhaps the horse is still influenced by a sort of biological clock, inherited from its ancient ancestors, that signals some groups to travel on, while others remain behind.

Today's horses, in any event, are not particularly territorial — possibly because their territory is in constant flux. But the pecking order remains paramount wherever they go, and becomes especially apparent at water holes. If a dominant stallion and his harem reach a hole occupied by a subordinate group, the latter herd will invariably withdraw, rather than risk a confrontation.

Once in possession of a water hole, the group's hierarchy is strictly observed. The stallion stands guard while the rest of his family take their turns, starting with the dominant mare. In arid districts, most harem groups will seldom stray more than two or three miles from the water source, returning to drink once a day.

Much of the remaining time is spent eating. A horse's digestive system is surprisingly inefficient for so highly evolved an animal. It requires that everything be thoroughly chewed before swallowing, and demands the most remarkable quantities of food. As a result, the horse's teeth are in action fully half the day, milling as much as thirty pounds of shrubs and grasses into a digestible pulp. This inefficiency leads to the frequently levelled charge of "over-grazing." Anti-horse factions claim that horses offer unfair competition to other animals occupying the same turf. In fact, so faulty a set of innards often allows entire seeds and grains to pass through intact. These emerge, nicely fertilized, and produce new crops more quickly than would otherwise be the case.

Major changes in the horse's diet are dictated by seasonal and regional factors. Grasses, reeds and shrubs are fair-weather mainstays. In winter, horses will resort to uprooting entire grass plants, eating sweet young twigs, or digging with their hooves to expose the roots. But these hard-scrabble techniques exact a toll. The quartz and silica content in the soil reduces tooth size, sometimes to the point where a horse has grave difficulty obtaining enough to eat.

Horses love to groom themselves, and the process takes many forms. The most common activity is rolling on grass, or in dust patches, mud and water. Wherever it occurs, the pecking order is once again observed, as the rolling horses jealously guard their grooming rights against anything that approaches.

Another method of self-grooming is scratching the neck and head against trees, rocks, fences and even the ground. Hooves are employed as well, to scratch the belly, while teeth are used to nibble where they can reach.

In addition, teeth come into play during the highly social act of mutual grooming. One horse will approach another, customarily from the front, signalling with eyes, lips and ears its desire to initiate the procedure. Once these overtures are accepted, the grooming partners begin with each other's necks, working their way down the flanks toward the tails, removing matted hair and dead skin from areas they cannot reach themselves. A particular horse will likely indulge in mutual grooming with only one or two of its fellows, leading observers to believe that the activity both solidifies a horse's place in the hierarchy, and serves as an expression of bonding and friendship within the herd.

The mating patterns of horses constitute the fullest expression of the ever-present pecking order. The scent of a mare in heat (or estrus) succeeds in attracting every stallion in the vicinity, compelling the dominant stallion to mount an almost constant vigil. He will attempt to ward off potential challengers by several means — first, by his habit of covering the mare's excrement with his own, as her waste contains an excessive quantity of estrogen. This reduces though fails to eliminate the likelihood of sneak attacks by keen-scented interlopers.

The stallion is well aware when his mares are in heat, but he will double-check the situation with an olfactory process known as flehmen. How this works is not precisely understood, but it seems to involve a sort of hyper-smelling. The stallion stretches his head and neck upward and out, curls back the top lip and sniffs with a vengeance. This is believed to expose secondary olfactory organs on the roof of his mouth, and may also bounce the scent back into his nostrils. Any unfamiliar odor can cause a horse to exhibit this behavior, but it is particularly associated with the presence of estrogen.

Mares generally come into heat in the spring, and will immediately mate several times with their dominant stallion (or, indeed, with any stallion that happens by). Their gestation period is eleven months, so that foals are born in the late winter or early spring, almost always at night. When birth seems imminent, the stallion will permit a mare to wander off to a secluded spot. This would seem to expose the new-born foal to predatory dangers, but, in fact, a marauder would likely be stalking the main herd. In any case, the stallion remains nearby, on call like any other proud father.

Within moments of its birth, the foal has been licked clean and encouraged to stand by its attentive dam. Shaking and swaying, it struggles up onto splayed legs within the hour. The next day, it is gambolling about on spindly shanks, gaining strength and stamina by the minute. Very quickly, it is capable of running with the herd, should flight prove necessary.

If the gangling colt is male, he has roughly three years of childhood and adolescence before he becomes an aggravation, if not a rival, to the dominant stallion. At about this time, bursting with equine hormones, he will be unceremoniously expelled from the family group.

Young stallions in this unenviable position tend to seek strength through numbers, banding together to form bachelor herds, acting out their own exuberant rituals as preparation for the day when they will be sufficiently powerful to claim a mare and launch a harem of their own. Not surprisingly, given the horse's passion for organization, a dominant stallion emerges within each bachelor herd. Swifter or larger than his fellows, he will be the first to make the leap into mature responsibility.

Young stallions take the art of play-fighting to extremes. What *seem* to be bloodthirsty battles erupt almost constantly, ending as suddenly as they began, and escalating into real combat only when the participants encounter another, rival bachelor herd, or attempt to poach the mares belonging to an already dominant stallion.

Indeed, our fondest image of the wild horse is that of the noble stallion, guarding the borders of his kingdom against all comers. But, as already noted, the horse is really quite accommodating when mere territory is at stake. In the Camargue region of southern France, for example, several harems coexist peacefully within the greater herd, and may even intermingle from time to time, returning to their original groupings later on.

Thus the vast majority of clashes between raging stallions of any age are in fact sham versions of the real thing. Horses are certainly more than capable of inflicting terrible damage with their teeth, and worse with their hooves. But, whenever possible, they are content to go through the motions of combat, declare a draw, and retire unscathed, their honor satisfied.

In a supremely practical vein, stallions will attempt to ward off intruders with ritual defecation. These "stud-piles" are, once again, more an expression of general dominance than the staking of a territorial claim. Stallions delight in relieving themselves on the spot where another male has performed his excremental chores, and the dominant male is careful to reserve his contribution till the last, topping off the offerings of subordinates within the harem or visitors from adjoining herds. In the American west, stud-piles serve as convenient meeting places, and reach considerable size.

Only when the issue of dominance remains in grave dispute will the mature stallion resort to a form of ritual combat, an active assertion of his rights.

Even these mock battles are an impressive sight, full of the most elegant, formal display. The stallions advance with arched necks, tossing heads, flying manes and stamping hooves. The mares, for whose favors the males compete, seem largely disinterested, and continue to graze casually nearby. But their coyness is deceptive; their eyes are focused on both forage and equine knights-errant.

Should the possibilities of ritual combat become exhausted, and the battle be joined in earnest, the mares will witness a truly dangerous struggle. Stallions are rarely killed in action, but some die a lingering death from injuries sustained—a broken leg or an infected wound that fails to heal properly.

Nor do superior size and strength ensure a stallion's victory. In her book *The Asiatic Wild Horse*, Dr. Erna Mohr recounts the story told by Dorschin Eregden Dagva, a young man from Mongolia:

> Dagva asserts that the Przewalski horses, when they come across a domestic mare in heat, will mate with them and, if necessary, fight the domestic stallion for the privilege of so doing. Despite their relatively diminutive size, their strength and survival skills will beat even the most powerful domestic stallions. He tells of one occurrence where part of a domestic herd, neglected by their owner, went wild, running into the mountains and resisting all attempts to recapture them, under the leadership of their stallion, well known to be one of the strongest in the area. When he had to fight a Przewalski stallion for his mares, he was virtually torn apart. Local herdsmen found him dying on the battlefield, legs broken, ears torn off, torn skin all over his body and with equally severe internal injuries. The fierce little stallion took his new mares off into the desert victoriously.

The domestic stallion in Dagva's story, at first glance, should have been able to outfight the adversary. He probably stood, if averages held, some four inches taller than his foe. He was almost certainly heavier and better fed, with a proven reputation. But, sadly for him, he had only recently regained his freedom. Pitted against a roving Przewalski, his scant months of liberty counted for nothing. The "fierce little stallion" triumphed, armed with a lifetime of day-to-day struggles and the savage inheritance, untainted by man, of centuries of life-and-death encounters.

A Camargue stallion displays the classic flehmen posture as he tries to determine whether a mare is in heat.

Right: Rubbing the neck and head against a convenient tree is a pleasurable self-grooming activity.

With lowered head and threatening
mien, this Camargue stallion drives
his mares away.

A Camargue stallion displays his
dominance.

A Camargue mare resorts to eating young twigs in winter.

Above: Rolling on the ground is a favorite form of self-grooming.

Overleaf: A mustang stallion remains behind his fleeing harem, ready to protect it if attacked.

This alert Przewalski employs its
well-developed senses of hearing and
sight. Note the ears pricked forward
and the characteristic light rings
around the eyes.

Right: These American mustangs
have just caught wind of the
photographer. The central horse
reacts nervously while the flanking
animals assess the danger.

High in the Pryor Mountains of
Montana, a stallion turns to face the
intruder while his harem melts into
the protection of the trees.

Camargue stallions go through the preliminaries of ritual battle while their mares look on.

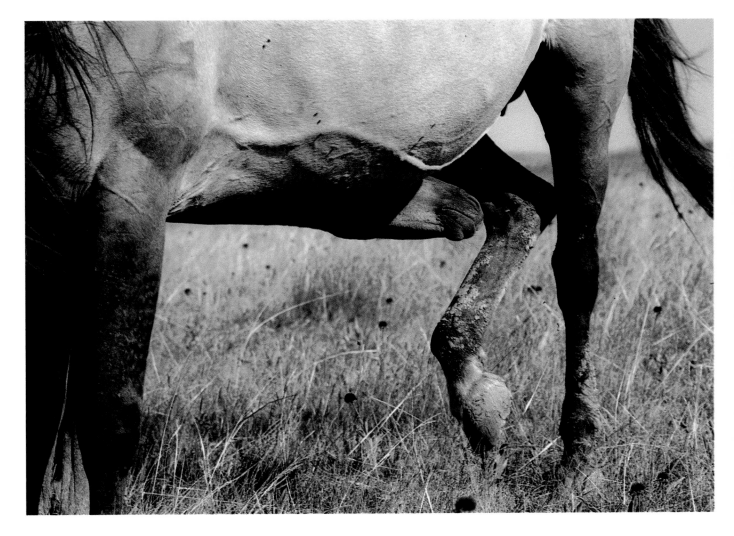

This mustang mare rejects her foal's feeding attempts.

A Camargue mare stands quietly for
her foal's first feeding.

The foal takes its first faltering steps in the warm glow of dawn.

Overleaf: Sable Island horses file in orderly fashion along a well-worn path.

3
THE PRZEWALSKIS OF ASIA

*I*n 1719, somewhere along the frontier between China and Mongolia, a Scottish doctor and nature enthusiast named John Bell chanced upon a herd of peculiar-looking horses. His published record, *A Journey from St Petersburg to Pekin* (1763), offered Western readers both a pleasing description of this previously unknown breed and an explanation of their impending doom:

> There is, besides, a number of wild horses of a chestnut colour; which cannot be tamed, though they are catched when foals. These horses differ nothing from the common kind in shape, but are the most watchful creatures alive. One of them waits always on the heights, to give warning to the rest; and, upon the least approach of danger, runs to the herd, making all the noise it can; upon which all of them fly away, like so many deer. The stallion drives up the rear, neighing, biting, and kicking those who do not run fast enough. Notwithstanding this

wonderful sagacity, these animals are often surprised by the Kalmucks; who ride in among them, well mounted on swift horses, and kill them with broad lances. Their flesh they esteem excellent food; and use their skins to sleep upon, instead of couches.

The western world received no further reports until 1870, when Colonel Nikolai Przewalski, a Polish-born officer of the Imperial Russian Army, invaded the Kalmucks' hunting grounds and shot a horse for sport. But, being of a curious bent, he shipped its skull and skin to the Zoological Museum of the Academy of Science of St. Petersburg (now Leningrad). There, in 1881, a biologist named Poliakoff leapt to the conclusion that he was dealing with something completely different. Wishing to enshrine both himself and the creature's discoverer, he named it *Equus przewalskii Poliakoff* and speculated on its ancestry:

> If our new species had more hair on the upper part of the tail, we would have a small dun domestic horse. His relatively coarse head is not so different from ordinary horses. And if, under the influence of domestication, it were possible for a fuller tail and a long mane, then I am prepared to believe that in fact, *Equus przewalskii* is the same animal whose ancestors were tamed by Stone Age people.

Poliakoff's belief was shrewder than he knew. In 1879, a Spanish nobleman named Marcellino de Sautuola was indulging his passion for archeology by prowling through a cave at Altamira, along the northern coast of Spain, accompanied by his daughter. Bored with the gloomy darkness, the little girl wandered out of sight. Suddenly her father heard her cry out, "Toros! Toros!" Rushing to rescue her from a herd of subterranean bulls, he followed her astonished gaze to the ceilings of the cave, only to find them covered with the paintings we know so well. In fact, the horses depicted in this and other caves are remarkable likenesses of what was to be labelled, two years later, a "new species." (The scientific community, sadly, poured scorn on Sautuola's contention that these were indeed Paleolithic paintings, and his discoveries failed to gain an official stamp of approval until 1902.)

What Sautuola rightly concluded was that the cavemen were producing strictly representational art — accurate renderings of what they hunted every day. Twenty thousand years ago, vast herds of Przewalski-like horses roamed throughout central Europe and Asia.

But, by the eighteenth century, when observed by Dr. Bell, they had been driven back to China and Mongolia—where, as he noted, they were still considered "excellent food." We know, from other sources, that in 1750 the Mongolian emperor's hunting parties numbered up to 3,000 beaters, and returned with as many as 300 carcasses in a single day. And, according to Erna Mohr, frontier guards were still hunting the Przewalskis for their meat in 1949.

Let us look more closely at this last vestige of another age. The body is colored a dun or strawberry roan; the mane is dark, short and stiff, with little or no forelock; the ears and muzzle are almost black. The nose, however, is highlighted by an oatmeal-colored patch, and a light band typically encircles the eyes. A dark dorsal stripe runs the length of the spine, connecting the bristly mane and the narrow, short-haired tail, which switches to longer hairs half-way down. Often, a series of stripes, or fingermarks, runs horizontally across the legs.

No doubt to deal with the harsh climate of its native land, the Przewalski radically changes its coat, if not its stripes, with the passing seasons. The summer coat is short and sleek, much like that of a domestic breed; but, unlike those of his tame relations, a Przewalski's mane and tail are included in the annual moult. With the coming of cold weather, the coat can grow up to six inches long. Sporting a tuft of eight-inch chin hairs, the Przewalski in winter resembles nothing more than a particularly large, shaggy and bearded donkey.

Most Przewalskis stand between fifty and fifty-eight inches high at the withers (12.2 to 14.2 hands, in the traditional measurement); their bodies are thickset and low-slung. The neck, especially that of a stallion, is heavy and powerful, supporting a head shaped like a truncated cone. Interestingly, in captivity, the Przewalski demonstrates extreme "plasticity"—meaning that each generation alters the shape of its head to resemble more closely that of a domestic horse.

No one who loves a graceful thoroughbred would find Przewalskis beautiful. They look, and are, pugnacious and irascible. But they are the last truly wild horses on the face of the earth, and what we perceive as shortcomings — their watchful, suspicious attitudes and ingrained ferocity—have ensured their survival. Even so, their numbers have dwindled to the extent that, today, only some 400 remain in all of the world's zoos.

Whether or not Przewalskis exist in the wild is open to debate. In 1926, the People's Republic of Mongolia passed laws protecting them from hunters—laws unenforceable in such a desolate region. The herds continued to decline though, as late as 1944, groups of fifty to a hundred horses were not uncommon. But the bitterly cold winters of 1948 and 1956 severely reduced their ranks. During the late 1950s, conservation measures seemed to permit a temporary increase, but subsequent contacts grew fewer by the year. In 1968, the Mongolian Academy of Sciences mounted an expedition which managed to confirm a sighting by local herdsmen—the last authenticated instance. In the summer of 1980, eight more sightings were reported; but three further expeditions, including one organized by the Mammalogical Society of China, failed to verify the presence of a single horse, with the result that most scientists now believe the Przewalski to be extinct in a wild state.

This may well be so. If natural perils were not enough, the horses' migratory patterns served them ill. Their regular travels took them, according to season, back and forth across the western end of the Gobi Desert—a vast, arid territory surrounded by towering mountain ranges, almost devoid of vegetation, and dotted with weirdly sculpted sandstone formations, much like the deserts of the American southwest. No one, at first glance, would covet such a land but this is, in fact, a portion of hotly contested frontier between China and Mongolia, the scene of ceaseless border skirmishes. Even if they were not intentionally hunted down, they must, at times, have had to run a gauntlet of stray bullets and artillery fire.

In this situation, strangely enough, lies our last faint hope for their survival. Perhaps the battles drove them off their normal course into some even more remote and impenetrable chain of mountain passes, from which they may yet emerge to astonish science.

In any event, the Przewalski lives on in captivity. Periodically, between 1898 and 1947, numerous horses were removed from their natural habitat, and transported to locations in Russia, Europe and the United States. The first breeding herd was established in Askania Nova, Russia, at a private zoo owned by a Baron von Falz-Fein. At first, many curators, monumentally unimpressed by their shipment of "ugly" horses, refused to accept them. (Indeed, many Przewalskis arrived looking much the worse for wear, with unhealthy coats and lopsided manes, lending them an even more mean-spirited appearance.)

As zookeepers got to know the rugged little animals, their attitudes changed. Unfortunately, they failed to reckon with the pitfalls of inbreeding. Resultant generations sickened and died and numbers began to plummet. By 1945, only thirty-one animals remained in zoos. By 1959, however, this total had risen to seventy, at which time Erna Mohr, with the cooperation of delegates to an international symposium in Prague, began an official studbook. This was later continued by Dr. Jiri Volf, of the Prague Zoo, with the result that, by 1980, 388 horses populated seventy-four collections worldwide. Today, the horses number about 1,100.

This remarkable recovery was qualified by an event that had taken place early in the century — the accidental inclusion of a Monogolian domestic horse in the breeding line. Only one group of Przewalskis in the United States escaped contamination by these genes. (While Przewalskis are a separate and distinct species, with a chromosome count of sixty-six as opposed to a domestic horse's sixty-four, they are all too readily interbred, producing a fertile hybrid with a count of sixty-five.)

Nevertheless, as a result of Mohr's and Volf's efforts, the situation has steadily improved, although much remains to be done before a relatively pure system of breeding lines can reassert itself, supported by regular "outbreeding" exchanges of animals between herds. This is now underway, thanks to the formation, in 1977, of the Foundation for the Preservation and Protection of the Przewalski Horse. Based in Rotterdam, under the direction of Jan and Inge Bouman, it seeks to coordinate information on a global scale — a task complicated by the uneven distribution of Przewalskis in captivity. As of 1978, fifty-four percent were housed in only twelve collections, and a mere nine zoos accounted for sixty-eight percent of the births. Still, a combination of the Boumans' data, the expanded studbook and research on the part of the zoos is slowly facilitating the establishment of a healthy captive population, marked by the fewest possible inbreeding defects.

The next, long-awaited step is upon us — the re-introduction of Przewalskis into the wild. Several locations in Ireland and New Mexico are under active consideration; and in Holland, through their foundation, the Boumans have designated forty hectares as a Przewalski reserve.

In addition, two other projects are currently underway. In the spring of 1991, six Przewalski horses were released into a 250-acre enclosure in Mongolia's Gobi National Park. If successful, the experiment will be expanded; the original six horses will be transferred to a 25,000-acre enclosure, and a further twelve horses will be released into the smaller enclosure, later to join the first six. Ultimately, if the group grows large enough, the horses will be released into the greater park area and left to their own devices in their ancestors' original grazing grounds.

In Europe, under the auspices of the United Nations Development Program, another herd of horses is being assembled from the most diverse gene pool possible—the horses in thirty zoos worldwide. They will be released into a small reserve. When they have started to function properly as a herd, they will be transported to China, for ultimate release into the Gobi Desert. We should rejoice at the prospect that the Przewalski, so recently only a short step away from tragic and total eclipse, will soon run free once more.

A stallion in silhouette reveals the powerful neck, stocky body and flared tail that are characteristic of the Przewalski.

A sociable family grouping typical of horses in the wild.

A group of inquisitive Przewalskis. The alert stallion stands guard on the right.

Two closeups of Przewalski heads
demonstrate the breed's plasticity.
The head above reveals the more
primitive characteristics of the
breed. The finer features of the horse
on the right more closely resemble
those of a domestic animal.

Overleaf: The classic driving posture of this stallion commands instant attention from the herd.

A young Przewalski in full shaggy
winter coat reaches around to groom
his tail.

This family, in the last rays of
sunlight, show their different moods
by the positions of their ears.

The mare on the left reveals the
characteristic dorsal stripe running
from the mane to the tail. Markings
on the younger animal are less
distinct.

A defiant stallion, his powerful
neck stretched, bares his teeth in
challenge.

4
THE
TARPANS OF
POLAND

*I*n ancient times, much of Europe was covered by magnificent forests — boundless expanses of enormous trees thrusting upward in competition for the sun, creating far below the green umbrella of their branches a vast twilight zone, covered with ferns and grasses, mushrooms and mosses, layered and overlayered with fallen leaves.

Warring native tribes and Roman legions tramped this eerie, vaulted wilderness, marching endless miles across the silent, spongy carpet of the forest floor. Only the strongest men remained, to put down roots of their own. Only the most tenacious species managed to survive hunters and the dwindling forest — the savage wildcats, the crafty sables and mighty bears all died out.

On the ground thrived the European bison and a horse first described by Herodotus, who wrote of small, white, wild horses living near the marshes of what is now the Ukraine. His is the earliest written reference — but Paleolithic cave art occasionally depicts a horse whose coloring far more closely resembles that of the forest

71

Tarpan than that of the Przewalski. Exactly when the Tarpans appeared remains unknown. They may have sprung from another group of feral horses of mixed ancestry; or, perhaps, like the Przewalski, they were a separate and untainted ancestor of our domestic breeds.

We do know, however, that their short, upright manes were black, as were their ears, eyes, muzzles, tails and dorsal stripes. The rest of the body was covered in summer with short, mousey-colored or ash-grey hair. In winter, the coat grew shaggy, white and bear-like—an effective natural camouflage amid the perpetual, dappled twilight of summer and the starker blacks and whites of winter. The Tarpans resembled a Przewalski in size and shape, but stood slightly smaller, with stallions measuring some fifty-three inches high.

By the end of the fifteenth century, the forest was slowly giving way to towns and fertile farmland. Its wildest outpost was an area in northwestern Poland, straddling the Russian border. The King of Poland, an avid hunter, declared this region a royal preserve. So keen was he to track and kill the bison that, between 1485 and 1492, he conducted his affairs of state from a woodland lodge. This building, a chateau distinguished by its white towers, was named Bialowieza, which in turn became the name of the forest itself.

The king and his courtiers paid little attention to the Tarpans, but nearby villagers, inspired perhaps by royal hunts, began both to feed upon the horses and to capture them for domestic use. Some three centuries later, in the late 1700s, a new threat arose. The end of the Russo-Turkish war brought to the adjoining steppes settlers who found that wild stallions were abducting their mares. Now outlawed, the Tarpans were mercilessly and efficiently hunted down —so efficiently that, by the mid-nineteenth century, they had become extinct.

The last eyewitness account of a true Tarpan, provided in the 1850s by a resident of the town of Zamosc, describes a group of horses in a neighboring paddock, "small in size as the peasants' horses, but compact, with thick but smooth legs, of great strength and of uniform black-mouse color. However, they were killed because of the expense of feeding them hay in winter."

Those sadly prosaic sentences sound the death-knell of a species that had covered Europe by the thousands, for centuries. Nor did the bison escape a similar fate. In Bialowieza, nineteenth-century monarchs had polished them off with such dispatch that scientists, recognizing their status as an endangered species, installed a small number in zoos just prior to the First World War. During that conflict,

German armies of occupation removed the last six hundred animals, leaving the European bison extinct in a wild state.

At war's end, Professor Tadeusz Vetulani was quick to investigate prewar reports of horses with distinct Tarpan characteristics in the vicinity of Zamosc. He was able to locate and purchase several of these domestic relatives, choosing those that most resembled their wild ancestors. These specimens were turned loose in Bialowieza, by now designated a National Park Forest. Vetulani carefully controlled the selection of breeding partners to isolate and emphasize the most Tarpan-like form and behavior patterns. As the herd increased, the animals indeed grew more and more primitive-looking, and the professor's experiment appeared to be an unprecedented success. At this time, as well, the bison began to make a comeback at Bialowieza, thanks to a small number of breeding animals retrieved from other zoos.

Then, in 1939, new legions tramped through the forest, as the *blitzkrieg* rolled into Poland. Hermann Göring, himself a hunting enthusiast, decided that Bialowieza should be reserved for his personal use, and that of other high-ranking Nazi officials. The horses, once again, were considered at most a nuisance. The strongest were removed to aid Germany's war efforts; the weaker were ruthlessly destroyed.

After the war, the few remaining Tarpan descendants that could be located elsewhere were returned briefly to the forest — then transported, in 1954, to the Institute of Genetics and Animal Breeding at Popielno, further north. Here, close to the Russian border, an amazing "back-breeding" program is taking place, under the direction of Dr. Magdalena Jaworowska. Its principal objective is to cultivate the strongly primitive features of the remaining *konik polski* (Polish horses). These traits include a robust and healthy nature, the ability to withstand harsh climatic conditions, a high fertility and reproduction rate and a facility for extracting maximum energy from available foods. The result is today's *konik polski*, which bear a close resemblance to their wild ancestors. Slightly larger than the true Tarpan, with a longer mane lying flat on the neck, they nonetheless retain most other important characteristics.

Several small herds exist, in stables and paddocks at the Institute, where they see occasional duty as riding or work horses. According to Dr. Jaworowska, two *konik polski* can haul a larger load than one traditional draft animal, while eating, between them, less fodder. In addition, their gentle nature is admirably suited to domestic chores.

Elsewhere, *konik polski* have been freed in a several-thousand-acre reserve in the forests of the Mazurian lake district, where conditions closely approximate the habitat of their forebears. Still others have been exported, in breeding pairs, to ensure their survival in zoos abroad.

One more group exists as well, in Bialowieza. Today, in regulated areas, visitors may walk this last remnant of the Polish forest. In winter time, the tracks of wild boar still dot the snow; and bison still lumber across the landscape. And, here and there, the keen-eyed observer may penetrate the natural camouflage of a small white horse, blending almost completely into its native background, as it moves silently among the ancient trees. The Tarpan, with a little help from man, is home at last.

This *konik polski* foal shows the dark mane and dorsal stripe to the tail that will turn dark as it matures. At this stage, the eyes and muzzle are darkly ringed. The mare on the left shows the more muted coloration of the mature animal.

A family group at rest in a clearing.

The horse on the right shows
delicate fingermarks on the legs, an
indication of returning primitive
camouflage.

Left: Two young *konik polski* rear up in mock battle in their woodland home.

This *konik polski* has not fully matured as the shorter mane and the light tail indicate. Its strong legs recall its primitive Tarpan origins.

5
PONIES
OF THE
BRITISH ISLES

Walk along the Ridge Way, a time-worn footpath cutting across southern England from a few miles north of Stonehenge toward East Anglia. A few miles from your starting point you enter the Berkshire Downs, where many of Britain's finest thoroughbreds have been produced. Perhaps you'll hear them as they approach, or feel the ground tremble beneath their galloping hooves. Spectral and awe-inspiring, they loom up out of the early morning mist and disappear, with only a fast-receding sound and a few clods of dew-laden earth to mark their passing.

Walk on, and you'll reach the three-thousand-year-old stone slabs of Wayland's Smithy, a Neolithic tomb. A mile further are the earthen ramparts of Uffington Castle, an Iron Age encampment dating from 400 B.C. Then, just below you on the down slope, you become aware of a strange design. The grass has been cut away, along with the shallow layers of earth, to expose the startling white chalk beneath. From where you stand, it is impossible to identify the shape; it is too immense. But from the air, the figure is revealed

81

to be a giant, leaping horse, 374 feet long by 120 feet high, crowned with a beaked and bird-like head. The White Horse of Uffington was carved by the Celts a hundred years before the birth of Christ; and, for as long as anyone can remember, the local people have gathered here every seven to ten years, singing the traditional songs as they cut back the encroaching grass and scour the chalkbase clean.

An ancient symbol — but horses were well established throughout the British Isles long before the coming of man. We know that the horse was here when the formation of the English Channel severed the last land bridge to Europe one hundred thousand years ago. Prior to that time, there must have been a great deal of activity, as European horses wandered to and fro, before those that became trapped offshore by the rising waters were left to pursue their distinct evolutionary fortunes.

Primitive Britons were quick to put the horse to use, in peace and war. Coins issued during the reign of Queen Boadicea show a symbol almost identical to the White Horse of Uffington — a stylized tribute to Epona, goddess of horses. Boadicea's warriors no doubt sought her favor as they rode against the Roman legions in 60 A.D. Their skins dyed blue with woad, they fought the better-equipped invaders from wicker chariots, pulled by teams of agile ponies — ponies that were already a crossbreed between horses imported by the Celts and local species those even earlier invaders found waiting on Britain's shores. With their size, strength and the ability to survive on short rations in an often harsh environment, the compact battle ponies of Boadicea's rebel army much resembled the breeds that remain today.

There are nine types of pony considered native to the British Isles, and we will examine three of them in some detail: the Exmoor, the Dartmoor and the New Forest strains. Others include the Irish Connemaras, whose ancestry is supposed to have benefitted from a dash of Spanish blood, courtesy of horses washed ashore from the shipwrecked galleons of the Armada. Perhaps as a result, they are among the most beautiful, rivalled only by the mountain ponies of rural Wales. Northern England's contributions are the Dales and Fells, which today serve, respectively, as trekking and harness animals. In northern Scotland and its offshore islands live the Highland ponies; and still further north, on the remote and barren Shetland Islands, are the shaggy, tiny, but exceptionally robust Shetlands. Fast learners, gentle and friendly, they provide an ideal first mount for small children — not to mention a source of endless fun for the

British cartoonist Thelwell. The Shetlands are believed to have occupied their storm-lashed homeland for two thousand years, and to have decreased in size in response to its harsh climate and sparse browse. Today, however, most of them are bred elsewhere. Horse owners, from time to time, have attempted to improve their stock with infusions of Shetland fortitude.

Let us begin our detailed coverage with the Exmoors, perhaps the most primitive variety. Traces of similar ponies have been found in many portions of the globe, prompting Hermann Ebhardt, a German scientist, to formulate a fascinating theory. He believes that their North American ancestors were trapped for a lengthy period in Alaska, completely encircled by ice during a glacial transition. Many died, but the survivors, freed from their frigid prison by a changing climate, proceeded to march westward, all the way across Asia, through Europe and into Britain. Ebhardt has traced their steps, and found that, while in Alaska, they began to develop an extra set of molars, the better to cope with a diet of scant, coarse grass and bushes. Their escape took place before this process was complete; but today's Exmoors have, in their mandibular canals, the blood vessels and nerve fibres for a seventh, non-existent molar tooth — the only species in all the world to exhibit this trait.

Mind you, a bigger brace of teeth would have served them well upon reaching their destination. The moors of Britain can be at once the most desolate and the most starkly beautiful places on earth. Drystone walls connect the hills and dales, meandering as far as the eye can see, seemingly oblivious to natural boundaries, broken occasionally by rushing streams and by cattle grids that straddle the winding laneways. Small woods and copses dot the landscape here and there; and everywhere, beneath your feet, are the tufted, springy grasses that frequently, frighteningly, tremble and quake, with only the intertwined roots to prevent you from slipping into the bog below. On the open heights, the wind blows bitter cold, and ominous clouds seem barely out of reach. Snow, fog and chilling rain make survival in wintertime unlikely for any but the supremely well-adapted.

The Exmoors are just such a breed — very distinctive-looking animals with a maximum height of something over forty-eight inches. Their predominant color is black, with oatmeal-colored patches on the nose and pale bellies. The eyes, too, are jet-black, surrounded by mealy rings that create two false impressions. From any angle, the eyes appear to bulge out; and from the front, they seem to be slanted, lending a somewhat oriental look.

An Exmoor's winter coat grows rather long, and is marked, in any season, by ingenious natural watersheds — loops or whorls, that cause heavy rainfall to drop off before it penetrates the hair or streams down to areas prone to chafing sores. The tail root and its hair covering, especially in the winter coat, perform a similar func- tion in protecting the sensitive rump and dock area. This is particu- larly important for an animal that habitually turns its back to the wind and rain, in a land where the wind always seems to blow and the air is so damp that it appears to be raining much of the year.

Over the centuries, man has been quick to recognize the Exmoors' hardiness and adaptability. Frequent cross-breeding experiments have been launched, with predictably mixed results. At one time, so many males were removed for stud purposes that the breed came within an inch of extinction. During the Second World War, sol- diers in training on the moors succeeded in destroying considerable numbers, and many more were butchered for their meat. In the late 1940s, however, a studbook was begun, and a serious program launched to ensure a comeback. Now, the remaining Exmoors are "gathered" once a year — rounded up and driven to nearby home farms. Over a two-week period, new foals and prospective breeding stallions are closely inspected and evaluated. Only those display- ing the true Exmoor characteristics are released to join the herds; but the rest come to no harm, since these "rejects" are much in demand as riding and harness animals and are eagerly purchased by private buyers.

In at least one portion of Exmoor, the area known as Withypool Common, local farmers notch their ponies' tails, the better to iden- tify them at a distance. This process is repeated, many times over, in another region further to the east, where "Agisters" of the New Forest conduct their annual "drift," or roundup. Here, the notched tail offers proof that a horse's owner has paid the annual grazing fee, and identifies which part of the 67,000-acre preserve the animal may browse in during the coming year.

With typical British incongruity, the New Forest is very old. The first written record of ponies there appeared in the Forest Law of King Canute, dated 1016—by which time the "commoners" (those with land holdings in and around the forest proper) already enjoyed a number of long-established rights, with grazing privileges upheld by a crown-appointed officer, the "Verderer." Until 1815, the forest was a royal hunting ground, but the Court of Verderers (England's second-oldest legal body) remained in force, as it does today.

Driving west from Southampton, you soon encounter the forest's northern boundaries — perimeter fences broken only by cattle grids. Frequent signs warn of ponies on the road. At night, the small, dark horses may not be visible until it is too late, and one of an Agister's least pleasant tasks is to put down wounded animals.

Today's commoners pay remarkably little for grazing rights (as well as the services of the Agisters, who remain on duty round the clock). In 1981, the annual fee was increased to ten pounds per animal, a fee collected at the autumn drift, where the animals are brought to central points, dewormed and branded. Some ponies are highly reluctant to lose their freedom, even for a day, and successfully evade capture by retreating deep into the bogs, moors and woodlands.

Still, the boundary fences allow authorities to exercise maximum control over the New Forest breed. A central registry examines all the stallions, and culls those foals that fail to meet requirements set by the New Forest Pony and Cattle Society: a maximum height of just over fifty-six inches, and a standard coloration, with no piebalds or skewbalds allowed. Such rigid standards, however, were not always in effect. Several attempts have been made to "improve" the breed, by introducing domestic stallions. But, visiting the forest in wintertime, you are forced to wonder how a diet of holly, ivy, brambles and gorse must have struck an animal accustomed to hay and oats.

Until quite recently, the New Forest ponies worked hard for a living. Farmers used them as pack animals; south-coast smugglers spirited them away to assist in transporting stolen goods. Some lived out brief and terrible lives as pit ponies in the coal mines; and, during the Boer War, the New Forest Scouts departed for South Africa mounted on local horses. But the breed's agility and versatility have been put to other, more pleasant uses. Competing with thoroughbred horses in both long-distance and jumping events, they have frequently proved more than a match for the larger animals.

West of the New Forest, almost due south of Exmoor, lies the fog-shrouded wilderness of Dartmoor. Here, too, roaming herds of ponies still thrive, as they have done since the days of King John.

Writings dated 1012 and 1296 make specific reference to their presence, and to the grazing privileges accorded local farmers.

To walk across the lonely moor in bad weather brings new meaning to the word "exposed." A sense of unease pervades the atmosphere, as visions of the Hound of the Baskervilles leap unbidden to your mind. Nearby is the massive greystone prison, a maximum security institution for the most dangerous offenders. Dartmoor seems an eerie place, a place to flee from late on a troubled night.

But, tucked away in sheltered hollows, you may find another, more welcoming side. Here are the tiny hamlets, clusters of warm and cosy houses nestled for protection against the sweeping winds. Here, in winter, the Dartmoor ponies come down from the high ground, to feed on emergency rations in their home meadows.

The ponies are no longer a pure breed, although their ancestry is fully registered and documented. Certainly they have proved of vital service to the area. For centuries, they were the principal form of transportation on the moors. The Dartmoors have suffered considerably from mankind's tampering, beginning with a major cross-breeding program in 1898. By 1902, they were banned from running free in attempts to purify the strain. In 1924, the maximum height was established at just over forty-eight inches, despite the introduction of "The Leat," a half-Arabian, half-Dartmoor stallion. Only eight of his offspring were registered in the studbook but almost every Dartmoor pony alive today can be traced directly back to him.

In the late 1920s and 1930s, another cross-breeding scheme, aimed at producing polo ponies, played further havoc with the Dartmoor strain. By this time, inbreeding had begun to take its toll so that, by the outbreak of the Second World War, the number of registered ponies had plummeted to 110, all in a single herd. Their owners were forced to dispose of a hundred animals — the sad results of twenty years' misguided intervention — and today's ponies have been developed, each and every one, from the remaining ten. Frequent crosses with Shetland stock have retained the Dartmoors' hardiness and compact stature. However, the studbook is closed, and at the October drifts many of the rejected foals go not to private purchasers, but to the slaughterhouse. Dartmoors, however, remain in demand and they have been successfully exported all over the world. Several breeding herds are developing in other countries, particularly France, where the goodnatured and versatile Dartmoor is very popular.

If the Ridge Way continued westward, it would pass yet another enormous symbol some thirty miles distant, carved into the slope of Bratton Hill. This is the White Horse of Westbury, and the story of its transformation closely parallels that of some British ponies. The original horse was phallic in the extreme, and boasted both a saddle and a splendid tail, ending in an upturned crescent, a motif that was supposed to bring good luck, much like our present-day horseshoe. It almost certainly dated from a very early period, and ought to have been left alone to age with grace, much like its spiritual twin by Uffington.

Such, however, was not to be the case. In 1778, a surveyor employed by Lord Abingdon, on whose land the horse was situated, took it upon himself to "improve the breed." This is the version we may see today — a very ordinary-looking eighteenth-century horse, bearing little resemblance to its pagan forebear. In a spirit of rampant modernism, local authorities have gone so far as to pave over the revised outline, sparing people the trouble of clipping back the grass. Like its living counterparts, the Westbury Horse fills concerned onlookers with a sense of waste — a longing for what might have been, had not man elected to intervene, to the horse's eternal detriment, and our eternal loss.

Left: The bedraggled winter coat of this Exmoor shows the exaggerated whorls which help to shed the rain water before it reaches the tender undersides.

A small family of Exmoors mingles freely with the cattle on the moors.

The coats of these Exmoor ponies
(*left* and *above*) are different shades
but all have coloration that is
reminiscent of the Przewalski: dark
manes, tails and lower legs, pale
bellies, mealy muzzles and light
rings around the eyes.

The New Forest ponies are
well-adapted to the damp chill and
meagre forage in the winter months.
Here, two shelter from a heavy
snowstorm.

Venturing from the shelter of the trees, this New Forest pony with snow settling on its back looks for a likely spot to uncover the sparse grass.

These two New Forest ponies resort
to eating holly (*above*) and prickly
gorse (*right*) in a severe snowstorm.

The clipped tail of this New Forest
pony tells the Agisters where it
should be grazing and indicates that
its owner has paid its grazing fee.

Four Dartmoor ponies flee from an
approaching car at the entrance to
the moor.

An older Dartmoor annoyed by a
frisky younger pony, stands its
ground (*above*) and (*right*) threatens
to bite.

Left: In winter, most Dartmoor
ponies come down from the higher
exposed ground to their home
meadows.

A sure-footed Dartmoor picks his
way through a winter stream.

Well-adapted to its bleak moorland
home, the Dartmoor is able to
survive in a terrain that is alternately
rocky and waterlogged.

Short, stocky and good-natured, this
Dartmoor reflects the best qualities
of the breed.

Formerly a Celtic tribute to Epona,
goddess of horses, the White Horse
of Westbury was given a more
pedestrian design in the eighteenth
century.

6
WHITE HORSES
OF THE
CAMARGUE

*C*enturies ago, the Rhône River flowed from its origins high in the Swiss Alps, down through south-central France and into the Mediterranean Sea. Whipped on by the Mistral, a frigid northerly wind, its waters tore deposits of soil and silt from the river banks, carrying them onward in a muddy torrent. Only where the river waters clashed with the turbulent sea did the opposing forces cause these deposits, halted in their progress, to settle slowly to the bottom and remain.

Over the course of hundreds of thousands of years, an ever-shifting delta appeared where river met sea. Now the waters overwhelmed their banks, spreading across an area twenty miles wide. Mingling and blending, in constant flux, they transformed the landscape. Ever so slowly, an island emerged in mid-delta, and still the river spread, its waters dividing into a multitude of smaller streams through new and fertile land.

By the time Julius Caesar's Sixth Legion occupied the nearby town of Marseilles, the Île de la Camargue had become the lush plain it

107

remains today, bounded by the Rhône's two major streams, and teeming with wildlife. Thousands of ducks inhabit its ponds and lakes; gulls and cormorants, owls and hawks, stately heron and decorative flamingos find refuge amid its vast marshes. Rabbits and hares abound; foxes, badgers, martens, polecats and weasels prowl the countryside; and wild boar, hidden during the daylight hours, root stealthily about at night.

Two other animals also make the Camargue their home: the black bulls and white horses which, we know, were in the region well before the Roman soldiers came. Their exact origins remain obscure, as does the precise term of their residency; but, once again, the cave paintings provide a vital clue, depicting horses that bear a marked similarity to modern-day Camargues. In height, today's horses closely resemble the Przewalski and the Tarpan, suggesting a common ancestral bond; but the Camargues, to some degree sealed off from the world, have developed unique characteristics. The fact that they are equally at ease in marshes and ponds or on dry land argues for a lengthy period on-site. Even their relative isolation has not guarded them from the sporadic introduction of other blood-lines though, since 1968, they have received official recognition as a separate breed.

For many years, horses have played an important part in the daily life of the *Camarguais*, superb equestrians with longstanding traditions. Their extremely comfortable saddles — high and heavily padded, rising in the rear to a sort of backrest — are very similar to those employed by armored knights who rode to battle from the walled city of Aigues-Mortes, a jumping-off point for the Crusades. So are their half-basket stirrups, which ensure that a rider's feet will not be caught, in the unlikely event of a tumble from so secure a seat.

Today, the region's *manadiers* (ranchers and breeders) and trident-carrying *gardians* (mounted herdsmen), none of whom would be caught riding a mare, rely on local stallions for many of their tasks. All year round, *gardians* may be seen throughout the Camargue and nearby Languedoc, driving champion bulls through the town streets on their way to the *course libre*, a non-lethal bullfight, where the only blood likely to be shed is that of *razeteurs*, agile youths dressed all in white, who attempt to pluck a rosette from between the horns of a charging beast. The *Camarguais*, at work or play, are fiercely proud of their traditions, and stubbornly resist the winds of twentieth-century change.

Part of the Camargue, including the seventeen-thousand-acre

Etang de Vaccarès — a lake with an average depth of three feet — is presently a nature reserve, dotted with breeding stations for both horses and bulls. To the north and west of the lake, a region known as la Petite Camargue, irrigation of the sandy soil yields bountiful crops of grapes and rice; while to the south-east, low-lying flatlands are flooded with seawater and allowed to dry out, producing a valuable harvest of salt. Close to this latter area is the Biological Research Station of la Tour du Valat, founded in 1954 by Dr. Luc Hoffmann, whose commitment to the preservation of the Camargue's wildlife — particularly its birds — is both long-standing and prodigious. Here, since 1973, when fourteen animals were released in the sanctuary's pastures, a study program headed by Dr. Patrick Duncan has focused on Camargue horses at semi-liberty.

These horses were a mixed group of males and females, both mature and immature. Characteristically, they were sturdily built, with an average height of between 52 and 56 inches, squarish heads, and large hooves that enabled them to maintain a footing on the marshy terrain where their favorite water plants grew. All had been previously used to produce foals for sale but now they were to be left almost entirely alone, apart from observation at a distance.

Dr. Duncan's team carefully charted their adaptation to new-found independence. At first, the horses continued more or less as before, most of the males living in the breeding herd with the mares and foals. Then, as the young males matured, the herd's wilder instincts became gradually more pronounced. The dominant stallion, Darius, expelled subordinate males from the band, and began to assert his authority. But after three years, several females were poached, to form new harems. Studies at this time showed that other stallions, on guard against their rivals, were herding their families about twice an hour.

Another two years later, the original group had grown to fifty-six, and contained a bachelor herd. Sad to say, Darius has lost his dominance of late, along with all but one of his mares. Indeed, he and his remaining favorite seem to have settled into the role of honored elders during their later years.

Researchers verified that, while some foals may be born as early as January, the majority appear later in the spring. Most arrive at night and, with plenty of encouragement, are standing within the hour. The rest of the harem gather round, but are not usually permitted to sniff the new arrival until it is strong on its feet. All foals are born black, red or brown, but gradually change color, becoming all-white between the ages of three and seven.

Shortly after giving birth, the mares come into heat again, taxing the over-extended stallion's energies. He must mate with each one several times, or risk losing her to eager challengers. For both males and females, spring is the season to rebuild their strength, after the winter's sparse fodder. Fortunately, the Camargue's lush plantlife bursts forth just in time to replenish their food supply.

As soon as the foals are confident enough to leave their mothers' sides, they take to their heels, gambolling together across the fields, stopping occasionally to nurse, or, suddenly exhausted, to drop in their tracks and sleep. Now several mares, less anxious than before, take turns watching over a group of foals, rather like supervisors at a day-care center. Often, a hungry foal will approach someone else's dam, only to meet with a brisk rebuff. Suitably chastened, the foal backs off submissively, clicking its teeth with lips pulled back, to signify appeasement. These proprieties observed, the mare returns to its grazing, and the foal bounds off in search of its rightful mother.

In addition to the foals, May brings other visitors to the Camargue. Some are welcome — the gypsies, who gather from all over Europe, ten to twenty thousand strong, to celebrate the feast of Sarah, their patron saint. Others are most assuredly not — the swarms of blood-thirsty horseflies that settle in for the next six months, accompanied by midges and mosquitoes. As the summer's heat increases day by day, the Camargue's marshy pastures cake and crack, and its pondwaters turn filthy and brackish, providing ideal spawning grounds for insect life. The horseflies' unrelenting presence drives the horses to bare ground with no suitable graze, but where the slightest wind will help to drive off their tormentors. They also cluster in larger-than-normal groups, swishing their tails and stamping their feet to ward off the ceaseless attacks. Studies have shown that the larger a group, the fewer the insects per horse, so that a system of mutual defence appears effective to some degree.

Another intriguing theory under consideration at la Tour du Valat may explain the Camargue horse's unique ability to turn all-white in adulthood. Comparisons of the number of horseflies and mosquitoes on dark and light horses reveal that the dark ones score consistently higher counts — a distinction explained by the fact that dark colors are known to be more attractive to passing insects. It seems possible that the horses' change of hue is therefore an on-going evolutionary adaptation, enabling them to better withstand one major drawback of their environment. If so, we may one day see Camargue foals appearing white at birth.

111

WHITE HORSES OF THE CAMARGUE

As the long, dry summer draws to a close; the Camargue is cloaked in vibrant color. Huge flocks of migratory birds prepare for their journey south, and the mosquitoes seem to redouble their onslaught, until dispatched by the first frost. The horses begin to sprout their shaggier winter coats, in readiness for the harsh weather and the poor grazing that lies ahead.

When the first winter Mistral sweeps down the Rhône Valley, the horses turn their backs, tails drooping down between their legs. The Mistral can blow for days at a time — a steady, bone-chilling gale that bends the long marsh grasses, lashes the horses' manes back over their faces, and whips the shallow ponds into wavelets that may become sudden ice-sculptures overnight.

When the winds drop at last, it feels at first as though something vital is missing. The silence is briefly deafening. Then, the sounds of the Camargue — the peculiar croak of the tree frogs, the joyous birdsongs, the snorting of bulls and horses, grazing side by side — quickly reassert themselves. The horses break shelter and resume their daily patterns. Fifty to sixty percent of their time is spent eating, especially in winter, when their normal foodstuffs are in short supply and of decreased nutritional value, and they may resort to eating twigs and bark from the wind-blown trees.

The Camargue is a magic region at any time of year, especially so at night. When the Mistral has ceased its seemingly endless roar, an almost tangible enchantment spreads all around you. The sky sparkles clear and black, and from your wooden observation platform, set on stilts where the muddy flats of the Etang de Vaccarès begin, the impression of timeless suspension is undeniable. Then, toward dawn, when the cold intrudes upon your dream and a ghostly mist arises from the plain, the dim outlines of white horses move silently to the water's edge to drink, as they have done for centuries before, and another day begins.

Alert and curious, this group of adult
Camargue horses is unalarmed by
the presence of humans.

The dark spots on the coat of this
horse in repose reveal that it has not
yet reached full maturity. The coat
turns pure white between the ages of
three and eight years.

A family near Aigues-Mortes wades in search of succulent water plants.

Right: A horse silhouetted against a muted winter sunset and the endless flat horizon of the Rhône delta.

A hungry mare and foal brave the windlashed open pasture in search of food.

In winter, Camargue horses are reduced to eating poor grass and young twigs.

Overleaf: Powerful and sure-footed, a group of Camargue horses gallop through reeds and water.

Camargue foals may be born black,
red or brown. The white star on the
forehead of this foal, not yet two days
old, suggests the changes in color
that are to come.

This unusual-looking yearling, with
its short, pale mane and tail, bears
little resemblance to the mature
horses.

Left: Two young stallions in a playful mood.

The play turns more serious as the stallions fall to their knees and bite at each other's legs.

An intruding stallion is repulsed.

Two mares in quiet companionship.

A stallion displaying this driving
posture is not to be ignored.

Ritual posturing and threats may be
enough to resolve this argument
between stallions. If it ends in
combat, the risk of injury is high.

Left: Teeth bared and hooves flashing, two stallions rear up in combat.

Sheltering quietly, their rumps to the wind, these horses are bathed in the pale gold light of a late winter afternoon.

7
THE HORSES
OF
SABLE ISLAND

*T*he icy Labrador Current sweeps south past Newfoundland, into the Gulf of St. Lawrence, then swirls eastward in enormous eddies, out through the Cabot Strait, before curving down along the continental shelf and the eastern seaboard of New England. Out near the edge of the shelf, about 150 miles east of Nova Scotia, it suddenly converges with two other forces. Here the St. Lawrence's river water breaks through at last into the open sea; here, too, the much warmer Gulf Stream deviates from its normal course, veering in toward land. Ever so slowly, century by century, the sands deposited by the last glaciation have been pounded and shaped into a wind- and water-sculpted island, twenty miles long by a mile and a half wide. Slightly crescent-shaped, its two arms fade into long, spindly points running north-east and north-west. Its contours change from year to year, at the whim of wind and weather; but, beneath the waves, it is in fact anchored by a much larger sandbank measuring some fifty miles in length.

131

Transatlantic navigators first identified Sable Island in the year 1500, and quickly learned to fear its treacherous currents, impenetrable fogs and towering waves. Since that sighting, more than 500 recorded shipwrecks have claimed in excess of 11,000 lives. Sailors who'd come too close for comfort were given to wild exaggeration, reporting that Sable was 200 miles long, capped with dunes 800 feet high, but the plain truth is impressive enough. Storm-tossed waves can reach a height of sixty feet, breaking far inland and contaminating the few freshwater ponds. The only form of vegetation is the coarse, shallow-rooted marram grasses — aromatic and plentiful in summertime, but sometimes covered by snow or sand when winter comes. For most of the summer, Sable is fog-enshrouded, a condition produced by the three converging currents, with their radically different temperatures. Rugged and foreboding, Sable has long defied man's efforts to alter or subdue its mysterious presence.

And yet, it is the home of another band of wild horses — diminutive animals with unruly, wind-swept manes that appear and disappear atop the dunes in ghostly silence, just as the wrecks of long-lost ships are exposed one day and covered the next by the ever-shifting sands.

No one is certain how they came to Sable. One theory suggests that their ancestors swam ashore from the wreckage of a French ship, driven aground in the 1600s. Others believe that they were imported by some distant colonialist, or that a lighthouse keeper wanted equine company on his lonely vigil. Another, more specific version credits Thomas Hancock, a Boston merchant who, it is said, imported a herd in the mid-eighteenth century to serve as food for the survivors of shipwrecks. Whichever version we accept, it is known that the horses have been on Sable for somewhere between 250 and 400 years, or a minimum of forty generations.

From time to time, man has attempted to alter Sable's ecology, with occasionally bizarre results. Tree-planting schemes have come and gone, foiled by the fierce, sand-bearing Atlantic winds that cut exposed flesh in minutes, and effectively prune mere saplings back to nothing. In the 1880s, an influx of rats from sunken ships threatened to take over the island. The Canadian government's solution was an army of cats, under whose care the rats were eliminated. Their work complete, the cats proceeded to multiply, at which point, baffled authorities sent in packs of dogs. Somewhat later, rabbits were introduced; but, like the cats, they simply over-ran the territory, and a second wave of cats was summoned to control them.

This sort of thing might have gone on indefinitely, had not a band of foxes solved the problem at one fell swoop.

Sable Island is the home of other, more legitimate wildlife. For many years, biologists puzzled over the mating habits of the Ipswich Sparrow, a bird that populated the eastern seaboard from New England to Georgia, but seemed never to lay eggs. In 1894, its nesting grounds were discovered in the dunes of Sable Island. Here, too, bands of grey seals return every year to breed, before setting off on their ocean voyages.

The behavior patterns of a Sable Island horse depend entirely on the season. In summer, on days when the sun burns off the seemingly perpetual fog, and the marram grasses are at their most nutritious, you might observe a family group, galloping joyfully along the flat white beaches that stretch on to meet an almost indiscernible horizon. Others wade into the ponds to drink, and eat the marshy reeds — while on the ridge of a nearby dune, another family files by, silhouetted against the sky. First come the mares and straggling foals, followed by the watchful stallion, sniffing the air in wary concentration.

During the storms that arise at any time of year, the horses huddle together for protection, rumps turned to the wind and rain, seeking what shelter they can in the lee of the dunes. In wintertime, the cruellest months, the horses that manage to survive are those most adept at locating the shrunken grasses, buried beneath blown sand, snow and frozen seaspray. Now they must break through ice to reach the pondwater, or dig down through the sand to hidden springs.

Man has not been keen to reside in such a harsh environment. In the early 1880s, a lifesaving station was established to keep watch for vessels in distress. Later that century, a number of lighthouses, long since abandoned, made their appearance. Today, their remnants stand almost in the ocean, the land on which they stood washed away by the incessant tides. During the Second World War, a Morse code relay station was established, along with a weather station presently manned by the Canadian government's Atmospheric Environment Service. All around the clock, every day of the year, it beams back hourly reports of local storms to an anxious mainland. A small cluster of modern houses, built to accommodate its personnel, stands inland from the new, automatic lighthouses that warn off unsuspecting mariners. The houses erected by former inhabitants are deserted ruins, often buried to the roofline by wind-driven sands. The few remaining panes of glass are frosted and opaque, ground down by abrasive sand particles. An onlooker can only marvel at how the horses, even with their wooly winter coats, can possibly withstand such terrible conditions.

Many, in fact, do not. During the winter of 1891, the earliest year for which records were kept, between seventy-five and a hundred horses died. Nor have matters improved in this century. In the fall of 1958, the herds totalled 300 animals; by the following spring, almost half had perished. By this time, however, an aroused public had become acquainted with their plight. (The government had in fact attempted to help matters, by dropping tons of hay from Royal Canadian Air Force search-and-rescue planes. But, according to weather station operators, the horses had refused to eat the food, because they detected the alien scent of human hands.)

Unable to devise another remedy, the government's Crown Assets Disposal Corporation decided to remove the survivors. It declared them to be "surplus goods," for sale to the highest bidder. Howls of protest rang through the nation's capital, as the normally compliant Canadian public demanded a stay of eviction. So it was that in June 1960, Prime Minister John Diefenbaker issued an official proclamation. In part, it read: "The horses of Sable Island and their progeny will not be removed, but left unmolested to roam wild and free as has been their custom for centuries."

Today, the horses remain, even though the winter of 1979, the worst on record, saw their ranks reduced to a total of 150 once again. What will become of them and their descendants remains in doubt. Dune restoration projects are being carried out, in efforts to stabilize the marram grasses. If successful, these will at least increase the horses' natural food supply. But the recent discovery of massive offshore oil and gas deposits, practically within sight of Sable, poses a far greater threat than wind and weather. An accidental spill amid the swirling currents would certainly doom the fragile shoreline; our only hope is that technology will somehow be kept at bay, leaving the horses to combat the age-old rigors of their island home. The Sable Island horses have shown that, left alone, they can endure. With their numbers already up to 250, they serve as an ongoing example of the survival of the fittest.

Previous Page: Galloping across the grass-covered dunes of Sable Island.

Left: Seaweed is a nutritious though unusual dietary alternative in winter.

Above: Sheltering from the spring wind, this foal huddles close to its mother.

Previous Pages: Typical Sable Island terrain. Sparse tufts of marram grass help to bind the surface of the dunes in the background. The horses seek out richer grasses in and around a small freshwater pond.

The rigors of winter on Sable Island. This group (*above*) turn their backs to the snowstorm. Their coats heavily matted with snow (*right*), several horses venture out in search of food. During severe winters, many horses may die.

8
THE AUSTRALIAN BRUMBIES

*E*arly members of the horse family, world travellers though they were, failed to negotiate the land bridges that from time to time connected the continent of Australia with south-east Asia. The continent's European discoverers — sixteenth-century Spanish and Portuguese — though they found a remarkable assortment of native wildlife, soon noted the absence of large placental animals such as the horse. Without exception, the indigenous mammals were either monotremes (the platypus and other egg-laying animals), marsupials (the kangaroos, wallabies and koalas, whose prematurely born offspring are carted about in an abdominal pouch), or smaller rodents and bats. Mammals such as the horse were nowhere to be seen. Australia, in fact, remains the only continent in which scientists have been unable to locate fossilized evidence of bygone equine forms.

Horses first arrived aboard trading ships that landed on the western and north-western coasts in the late 1600s. These vessels came via the Cape of Good Hope, bringing with them Cape Horses and

Basuto Ponies—related cross-breeds derived from Arab, Barb, Persian and thoroughbred stock. Used to the harsh conditions of their South African home, they experienced little difficulty in adapting to a new-found land. Indeed, judging by records of the period, a good many were allowed to run loose shortly after their arrival.

Not content with the exotic species that awaited them, later settlers embarked on a series of extraordinary importation programs. As time progressed, a bewildering assortment of creatures — sheep and cattle; pigs and goats; foxes, rabbits and camels; donkeys, deer and water buffalo—were transported across the seas. Many escaped to the wild, with the result that Australia very soon enjoyed the dubious distinction of having more feral animals than any other country in the world. (Even the dingo, the so-called "wild" dog, is the descendant of domestic beasts.) These feral animals, as they bred and overbred, began to compete with the ever-increasing sheep for sparse forage and limited water. In turn, they came to be viewed as mere pests, fit only for wholesale slaughter. The horse, as we shall see, was to share this unhappy fate.

As the colonial settlements expanded, several varieties of horses were introduced to widely scattered districts, creating local hybrids. In New South Wales, the first wave of immigrants brought with them, in 1798, seven horses of largely Spanish blood. Subsequent shipments included Arabs and thoroughbreds, which, in turn, produced a cross-breed known as Walers. By 1821, their numbers had mushroomed to more than 4,500. These clever and agile mounts were a favored cavalry horse of the British armies in India. During World War I, they were to carry Allied servicemen across Europe and into the Palestinian desert. Though they deteriorated in time, becoming a type, rather than a breed apart, the domestic Walers were to some degree prized and recognized. The Brumbies—a catch-all designation for feral horses of any stripe—were not so fortunate.

In 1804, a horse breeder named James Brumby was seized with the desire to quit the Sydney area and join an expedition to Tasmania. When he left, he chose to abandon his entire stock. Before long, so the story goes, the term "brumby" was applied to stray horses throughout the entire continent. This explanation sounds suspiciously like an Australian tall tale. The word may be a corruption of "baroomby" — Queensland Aboriginal for "wild" — or Baramba, the name of a sheep station and creek in Queensland.

In any case, other settlers were soon to follow Brumby's example. During the gold rush of 1851, vast numbers of domestic stock were set free, as their owners went off in search of instant riches. By the late 1860s, "mobs" of roving Brumbies were the bane of the outback. About this time, the organized massacres began. In 1869, those hunters who could be bothered to skin their kill received four shillings for a hide, one shilling and sixpence for a pound of hair. Brumbies — "a very weed among animals," according to a chronicler of the day — were shot by the countless thousands. Others perished when their water holes were poisoned or simply fenced off, dooming the horses to die of thirst.

But the Brumbies were not extinguished. Those that survived grew crafty and shrewd, notoriously hard to track and capture, harder still to break and train (though, once caught, many proved to be excellent work animals). Physically, they almost defied description, coming as they did from so varied a parentage. Observers recorded a hundred variations. Some horses were ill-formed, with stunted bodies, splayed hooves and overly large heads; others appeared far stronger and more graceful, the result, no doubt, of superior bloodlines.

Today's survivors remain excessively wary, and to elude their pursuers have retreated even deeper into the vast outback, the plains of inland areas and the mountainous regions of north-eastern Victoria and southern New South Wales. In warm seasons, they take to high, barren areas, devoid of trees and other shelter; in winter, they descend to more protected valleys. In arid districts, they tend to graze during the night and early dawn, taking advantage of dew-covered grasses. Brumbies also dig for water, and at times excavate holes deeper than they themselves are tall. In other regions, they chew the bark off white box trees (a type of eucalyptus) to lick the sweet sap beneath.

The Brumbies' highly suspicious behavior patterns are best observed at a water hole. The herd approaches, always from downwind, sniffing the air for any hint of danger. At the water's edge, the stallion halts the group's progress, and advances alone to drink his fill, then stands guard while his subordinates take their turns. It is almost as if the Brumbies retain a memory of poisoned springs. More likely, however, they associate water with the presence of other perils, since the holes are a typical haunt of riflemen.

Relentless culling by several means has been the Brumbies' lot throughout this century. In a large-scale hunt, the horses are stampeded by planes, four-wheel-drive vehicles and even motorcycles into holding pens with V-shaped funnel wings. These wooden wings may be extended outward for miles, by stringing rope between trees or poles, and draping it with fluttering rags — a flimsy barrier that nonetheless contains the panic-stricken herds. Once in the holding area, only a handful of horses survive, to be broken as stock. Most are shipped to abbatoirs, to serve the petfood industry, or simply killed. In the past, gruesomely efficient methods were devised to be rid of unwanted or excess carcasses. Animals were mortally wounded, but left capable of running for several miles, only to die of their injuries at a sanitary distance. Other methods of killing in the wild have involved the maiming of a lead mare, whose cries for help attracted the loyal stallion. Rather than abandon her, he would remain, herding his subordinates, who could then be picked off at leisure.

It seems incredible that the Brumbies have not, in fact, become extinct. During the 1930s, two men were said to have shot 4,000 horses in a year. Shortly after the Second World War, another hunter accounted for 700 animals in a single night. And yet the Brumbies persist, in considerable numbers. In 1977, there were thought to be at least 165,000 spread throughout most of the countryside, particularly the central and north-central territories. The Snowy Mountains are a favorite area for them. Only one area is barred to Brumbies: the Cobourg Peninsula. Ironically, this is the site of a wildlife sanctuary housing some 500 Timor ponies, smallest of the Indonesian breeds, whose ancestors were imported 150 years ago to stock the district's long-deserted settlements.

Elsewhere, the Brumbies are still hunted down, the victims of stockmen's lobbies whose complaints echo those of American ranchers. They believe that Brumbies crowd out their herds of sheep and cattle, transmit all manner of parasites and disease, and occasionally poach domestic horses. If anything, the Brumbies' status is even more precarious than that of the American mustangs — in Australia, unlike the United States, the horse has no history of prior existence. But, as their numbers dwindle, public interest in the Brumbies has grown. Perhaps, in the near future, we will see the establishment of a refuge in some desolate region, where these resilient creatures, gone "from barnyard to bush," will be permitted to live in peace.

Previous Page: Though cautious, Brumbies will often allow humans to approach on horseback.

A healthy-looking mob of Brumbies turns tail at the approach of the photographer.

Generally treated as pests, Brumbies
have been consistently rounded up
and destroyed in great numbers.

9
MUSTANGS
OF THE
AMERICAN WEST

Seven centuries before Columbus crossed the Atlantic, an army of twelve thousand Moslems from North Africa, mounted on their fiery, part-Arabian Libyan Barbs, invaded and conquered Spain. The African horses — smaller, quicker and more sure-footed than the ponderous Norse Duns of the defenders — enabled the invading forces to out-ride their opponents, and proved the deciding factor in a victory that resulted in several hundred years of Moorish rule.

Both the horses and the riding style of their conquerors very quickly became a part of Spanish life. Traditionally, a heavily-armored knight had charged straight ahead into battle, counting on the impact of his lumbering steed. Now, however, the Spaniards hastened to adopt the superior tactics of their foes. This new riding style, which depended on controlling the horse by knee, thigh and hand, rather than by bridle, became known as *La Zeneta*, after one of the fiercest Moorish tribes. Telling someone he rode *a la Gineta* was the highest compliment one horseman could pay another.

151

But to employ this style, the Spaniards required smaller, more adroit mounts. They began to cross-breed their Norse Duns with the Libyan Barbs, producing the Spanish Barb, an animal that combined the best characteristics of all its ancestors: the fire and beauty of the Arabian; the compact, sure-footed speed and adaptability of the Libyan; and the strength and endurance of the Nordic warhorse. This new breed was named the Spanish Barb or Ginete (subsequently corrupted to Jennet). These were the animals that travelled with Columbus to the New World, under the most horrible conditions. Slung from their chests and bellies in the stifling holds of fifteenth-century ships, with only stale hay and brackish water for sustenance, the hardy Jennets not only survived, but, upon landfall, were ready for almost immediate service.

On his second voyage, Columbus brought with him fifteen stallions and ten mares. Five years later, in 1498, he transported forty horses more. Cortés, who valued a single horse more than the lives of twenty men, brought eleven stallions and five mares in 1519. These horses, a mixed breed of mixed colors, were the ones on which the Spaniards rode through much of North America and Mexico, spreading terror and amazement as they went.

Around 1540, De Soto set forth with large numbers of horses from the Spanish breeding farms in Haiti and several other Caribbean islands, heading for the Mississippi. At the same time, Coronado, inspired by the riches his predecessors had located in the south, struck out from Mexico through what is now Arizona, becoming the first white man to reach the homelands of the nomadic Plains Indians.

The several tribes that made up the American west's native population lived hard and precarious lives, tied to the migrations of their primary food source, the buffalo. Their only domesticated animal was the dog; and when they moved in pursuit of the buffalo herds, men, women, children and dogs alike were pressed into service as beasts of burden. Their meagre possessions were either carried or dragged along on travois.

The Comanche were astonished when they first encountered the armored Spanish riders. What were these large, fleet-footed animals, nearly as big as buffalo, but with long necks and shiny humps on their backs? When the humps dismounted and spoke in a strange tongue, revealing themselves as men, the Indians marvelled at them and the animals they rode. They called these new animals "magic dogs," and watched closely to see how the newcomers handled them. When the men remounted, the Comanche followed close behind, awaiting an opportunity to take the magic dogs for their own.

Not all the tribes had so fortunate an introduction to the Spanish invaders. Increasingly frustrated at finding no cities of gold en route, Coronado launched a long tradition of massacre by killing the Indians he suspected were misleading him. Not that wholesale butchery was necessary. The Spaniards were well aware of the effect they had on primitive peoples, and knew that the mere sight of their galloping steeds could inspire dread.

But their dominance was to be short-lived. Cautiously at first, then with increasing frequency and confidence, the Indians stole the Spaniards' magic dogs, mastering all the necessary skills and achieving a state of total harmony with their mounts with astonishing speed. Just as quickly, the horse transformed Indian life. Now, using only blankets for saddles, and ropes or thongs as bridles, a tribe was able to keep pace with the buffalo herds, ride in among them and kill them as required. Nor did the Indians have to move so often, since farflung herds were suddenly within a day's journey. But, when they did move, the smallest children were strapped across a horse's back, producing a generation of youngsters to whom horsemanship was second nature.

Whether or not they happened to be at war with one another, the Indians delighted in trading, and the horse soon spread from tribe to tribe. Horses were highly desirable trade goods, and easy to come by — more could always be stolen from the Spanish colonists. In fact, the Spaniards had begun to view their horses as a sort of insurance policy. As long as the Indians could steal them quietly in the night, the less likely they were to launch a full-scale attack on outlying settlements.

Before long, the horse had come to be viewed as a symbol of power and importance. Braves and chiefs kept two favorite mounts — one for hunting, the other for war, with any others reserved for status and trade. Horse stealing, too, became a standard measure of resourcefulness and skill. Young men would set off on foot, alone or in small groups, to prove their merit by rustling anything that moved. The more horses they returned with in the morning light, the higher their esteem would rise within the tribe.

Every tribe was quick to create its own legend, detailing how it had first received the horse, and devised its own ceremonial horse-dance to celebrate the event. The chant accompanying the dance performed by the Oglala Sioux speaks of a creature standing "at the centre of the earth," and of "a horse nation all over the universe." Each tribe, too, had distinct color preferences. The Sioux dance involved a hymn to sixteen horses, four of each color, which represented each of the compass points: white for the north, buckskin for the south, sorrel for the east and black for the west. The Cheyenne favored one type of horse above all others — the white-coated Medicine Hat, whose dark markings on the head and chest were thought to resemble a war-bonnet and breast-shield, rendering it sacred and protecting its riders in battle.

To the Nez Percé, a less migratory tribe living in what is now Idaho and southern Washington, the horse was more luxury than necessity. Nevertheless, they became fascinated by a type of horse with very peculiar markings, and concentrated on breeding only these animals in their homelands along the Palouse River. Named after that river, the Appaloosa has a solid-colored head, neck and chest, but a dappled rump. (The Nez Percé were not alone in their fascination; animals strongly resembling the Appaloosa appear in art all over the world, including the European cave drawings, and Chinese paintings dating from roughly 500 B.C.) We know, as well, that by concentrating on a single strain, the Nez Percé produced horses that stood from fifty-six to sixty inches high — eight inches taller than the animals kept by most Plains Indians, and almost as large as their ancestors, the Spanish Barbs.

With the exception of a few highly-prized animals, the Indians cared little for keeping their horses. More could always be stolen, with a degree of honor attached to the exercise. As a result, horses were allowed to wander off by the thousands. Naturally, large numbers failed to return. The land, the climate and the forage were hospitable to a free-range existence. This, after all, was where their distant ancestors had spent between fifty and seventy million years; where the tiny, jungle-browsing eohippus had evolved. The North American west was little changed in some 8,000 years, since primitive hunters and prehistoric holocaust had extinguished the equine family on its native soil. Now, free once more after the most brief captivity, the Indians' mounts prospered and increased, until vast herds of newly-feral horses streamed across the plains.

Some believe that the Spaniards called these horses *mestenos*, meaning that they belonged to stock growers. Another theory suggests that they were known as *monstrenco*, which translates as "rough" or "wild." Whatever its source, the name was soon Americanized to "mustang."

Most Indian tribes had been in possession of the horse since the late 1600s, and their riding skills proved a formidable obstacle as European settlers pressed westward across the continent. The immigrants brought with them (or bred in eastern regions) grain-fed, domesticated horses but these proved no match for the rough, unpampered animals ridden with such casual ease by nimble warriors, who thought nothing of sliding down a mount's side at full gallop and firing their bows with devastating accuracy.

By the turn of the nineteenth century. the American West was still relatively untouched; the herds of buffalo probably totalled more than sixty million animals. But the ever-advancing settlers, armed with new, improved weapons, began to threaten the Indians' nomadic way of life. The government viewed the tribes as an obstacle to progress, a savage people to be confined, at best, to their traditional hunting grounds. This policy was spearheaded by the army, which took care to confiscate the Indian ponies whenever possible.

In August, 1806, an officer named Sergeant Pryor was in command of a small detachment of soldiers, charged with delivering to a certain point a group of horses seized from the Indians. During this journey, the riderless ponies spotted a herd of buffalo. True to their training and nature, they chased and surrounded the herd, exactly as if they had been ridden to the hunt. Pryor's men succeeded in getting them under control — but shortly thereafter, in the mountains along the Wyoming-Montana border that bear his name, the Sergeant was outwitted by his captives, who bolted into the night, never to be recovered.

As the nineteenth century unfolded, and railroads spread across the west, the presence of hungry construction crews placed a new and fatal strain upon the buffalo. Railway builders employed full-time hunters, and many of the workers began to shoot whatever they saw, for recreation. Soon, the giant herds were in decline; and the mustangs, justifiably fearful of the noisy newcomers, began to retreat to higher ground, away from civilization.

Various legends started to spring up around the increasingly elusive mustangs. In 1832, Washington Irving offered the first account of a horse so fleet of foot, so unusual to behold and so infinitely desirable, that for the next half-century, every horseman of any repute felt compelled to have seen (if not have been an inch away from capturing) the Great White Stallion. More than forty different versions of the story survive, containing almost twenty slightly different names for this exceptional horse. His territory ranged from

Texas to Oregon, from Dakota to Mexico. In *Moby Dick*, Herman Melville interrupted his tale of a great white whale to offer the following account:

> Most famous in our Western annals and Indian traditions is that of the White Steed of the Prairies; a magnificent milk-white charger, large-eyed, small-headed, bluff-chested, and with the dignity of a thousand monarchs in his lofty, over-scorning carriage. He was the elected Xerxes of the vast herds of wild horses, whose pastures in those days were only fenced by the Rocky Mountains and the Alleghenies. At their flaming head he westward trooped it like that chosen star which every evening leads on the hosts of light. The flashing cascade of his mane, the curving comet of his tail, invested him with housings more resplendent than gold- and silver-beaters could have furnished him. A most imperial and archangelical apparition of that unfallen western world . . .

The stallion figured in many stories, appeared in many locations, and enjoyed a highly unlikely lifespan. But always he was white — and, no matter how accomplished his pursuer, the stallion remained at liberty. (It is tempting to make a connection between the stallion and his mythic brethren worldwide. Perhaps the unattainable white horse is a necessary part of our most deeply-cherished dreams.)

But the stallion was soon to be driven from his fallen paradise. In 1867, an event took place that was to forever change the western United States. When the Kansas Pacific Railroad linked Abilene and Chicago, the struggling cattle industry gained direct access to eastern markets. The region's economic future was assured, and the fate of the nomadic Indians and the buffalo just as effectively sealed.

Buffalo Bill Cody, who began his career as a railway-employed hunter, claimed to have single-handedly slaughtered thousands of buffalo in a single year. The railroads, to promote their services, advertised the fact that trains would slow down as they passed through buffalo country, enabling intrepid sportsmen aboard the cars to blaze away at shaggy beasts stampeding beside the tracks. A 200-mile section of the Kansas Pacific line became filled with the stench of rotting carcasses. By the closing decade of the nineteenth century, sixty million buffalo had been systematically reduced to several hundred. A distant government rubbed its hands, safe in the knowledge that the buffalo's destruction would compel the Indians to abandon their nomadic ways, settle down on reservations, and start to raise crops like normal people.

Another part of the government's plan involved increasingly vigorous confiscation of the Indians' ponies, which effectively removed their means of continuing a nomadic existence. The best were selected for use as cavalry horses; the remainder were either shot or sold. Cowboys knew that the finest cutting and roping horses were either Indian ponies, or mustangs captured on the range. Looks were irrelevant. What the cattlemen prized was an instinct and fluidity of coordination that allowed the horse to anticipate the reactions of both rider and steer. That, and the ability to survive under almost any conditions.

The mustangs, despite their Spanish ancestry, were not impressive horses to look upon. Shaggy, stunted and stubborn, they became objects of scorn to people familiar only with the elegant domestic breeds. They were called Cayuses — a term of contempt — after an Indian tribe, now extinct, that had been known for its vast numbers of horses. Mustangs that evaded capture by the ranchers came to be regarded, in many quarters, as a nuisance. Yet during the Boer War, when Britain demanded horses in unprecedented quantities, the lowly Cayuses proved themselves the best and most durable animals of all. Hundreds of thousands were rounded up and shipped overseas to this conflict just as, a few years later, they would be sent to serve in the First World War.

With these massive clearances, the time of the professional mustang-hunter had come. During the next few decades, countless horses were tracked down, rounded up and dispatched to various fates. Many animals were maimed and abused along the way. Who would care, knowing that most were destined to become fodder for the American pet food industry? No one did, and the mustangs' numbers dwindled by the year.

The problem, it seemed, was largely one of status. Without exception, all of America's horses were classified as either domestic or feral — never wild, since they were considered not to have existed prior to the arrival of the Europeans. This semantic trap left the mustangs in the position of horses without a country, with no agency responsible for their welfare. Indeed, the Bureau of Land Management (BLM), under pressure from both ranchers and mustang-hunters, did little to control their demise. Systematic removal of these unwanted pests allowed revenue-producing cattle unimpeded access to grazing lands, and generated further income from the sale of hunting licenses.

One person who opposed the government, waging a seemingly fruitless war for nine years to protect the mustangs' interests, was Velma Johnston, a Nevada woman. Outraged by what she perceived to be their indiscriminate slaughter, she lobbied unceasingly for government intervention. Her first success occurred in 1955, with the passage of a Nevada law prohibiting the use of aircraft to pursue wild horses or burros on lands owned by the state of Nevada. In a state where eighty-six percent of the land is federally owned, this measure did relatively little to prevent abuses — but four years later, with the aid of Nevada Congressman Baring, Johnston managed to have a similar bill passed at the federal level. All other methods of mustang-hunting remained legal, and continued to be employed; but the first step had been taken, and horses in the remote high country were rendered much safer as a result of Johnston's efforts.

Nor was Johnston alone in her concern for the mustangs' welfare. Since the early 1920s, Robert and Ferdinand Brislawn had been collecting and breeding horses with pure Spanish characteristics. Starting with wild ponies from several locations, including Indian reservations, they kept careful records detailing the lineage of their offspring. (Only when these animals died could the Brislawns confirm their true Spanish ancestry. Instead of the usual six large lumbar vertebrae, the pure Spanish mustang had only five.)

In 1958, the Brislawn brothers established the first Spanish Mustang Registry on the Cayuse Ranch at Oshoto, Wyoming. Free to roam throughout the area, these mustangs have become boldly inquisitive, used to the presence of visitors. If we could visit a portion of the spread, far from the Brislawns' ranch house, we would approach a treeless valley, marked by a central hill, and surrounded by a circle of smaller mounds, each about a hundred feet high. Here, just as the dawn begins to break, a half-dozen bands of mustangs gather silently, each family taking up its position around the perimeter.

Slowly, toward the east, a predawn glow comes creeping between the distant buttes and the spectacular Devil's Tower, a peculiar rock formation seen in the motion picture *Close Encounters of the Third Kind*. The first ray of sunlight touches the first darkened hill. Then, as more and more rays illuminate the other elevations, each group of horses is revealed in subtly different colors, players in a drama of their own devising. Motionless till now, the stallions spring to the beginnings of their ritual. Breath steaming in the frosty air, rearing and pawing the dusty earth, their screams rebound from hilltop to hilltop. Each takes up the refrain in turn, as the fully risen sun pours pink and golden light across the scene.

Finally, one stallion breaks the moment's unbearable intensity. With a cry, he plunges down his hillside, the harem in a breakneck gallop at his heels. Across the valley floor they go, toward another occupied hill. Its stallion and his family, taking their cue, break into a gallop of their own, sweeping down the slope. The scene erupts as six bands of horses crisscross the valley in a series of rushing waves, fully illuminated now in glorious reds and golds, their passionate screams filling the valley.

The area north and west of Oshoto is filled with placenames plucked from America's history books: Cody, Greybull and Buffalo, the Bighorn Mountains and the Custer National Forests. A few miles from the town of Lovell, straddling the Wyoming-Montana border, the Pryor Mountains climb skyward almost eight thousand feet, spanning thousands of acres of plateaux and canyons, valleys and meadows, rivers, forests and rocky cliffs. Wild horses were waiting here when the earliest settlers came — quite possibly, the descendants of those that escaped from the luckless sergeant some eighty years before. Unlike the Brislawns' mustangs, the Pryor Mountains horses are wary and cautious, shorter and stockier than their Spanish cousins, hard to spot and difficult to approach. The only access to their territory is on foot or by four-wheel-drive vehicle, and the prospects of your arriving undetected are minimal indeed. Creeping up from downwind, fondly believing yourself to be unobserved, you may suddenly get the impression you're being watched. Behind you, following at a curious distance, are the silent horses you were tracking scant minutes before.

Fortunately for the Pryor Mountains horses, the people who live on the plains below did not view their presence with disdain. In fact, the local residents' response was quite the opposite. In 1964, when they learned that the Bureau of Land Management planned to trap and sell off the two hundred mustangs that roamed the mountain peaks, their concern touched off an unprecedented surge of public sympathy and subsequent action.

Four years of legal battles ensued, serving only to delay the BLM's scheme. Then, in 1968, an American Broadcasting Corporation television producer decided that a battle between ranchers and the Department of the Interior — with the local ranchers, amazingly, on the horses' side — was more than newsworthy. Hope Ryden's investigations convinced her that neither of the department's arguments made sense. It planned to cede the range to hunting interests (who in turn planned to import bighorn sheep), and to free more grazing land for livestock producers — despite the fact that cattle do not graze that high, and that sheep prefer even loftier ground. Her coverage prompted a flood of mail to both the network and the BLM, as a crusade to save the horses from the slaughterhouse reached national scale.

The American Horse Protection Association, the Humane Society of the United States, and concerned citizens everywhere joined local forces in the struggle. Finally, an advisory committee was formed to weigh the conflicting claims. Its findings recommended that the Pryor Mountains horses be given priority on these public lands, perhaps the first time that an official body had acknowledged that wild horses were suitable to any portion of the United States. But the committee's findings failed to gain effect. Elsewhere, the situation remained unchanged: all unbranded horses belong to the state in which they lived, and feral horses didn't belong anywhere. The pet food business continued as usual. By 1967, the BLM estimated that only 17,000 horses remained; and in 1970, other experts stated that if the decline continued at then-current rates, the mustangs would be extinct within a decade.

That same year, however, the publication of Hope Ryden's book, *America's Last Wild Horses*, brought new vigor to the debate. Readers responded in phenomenal numbers; a massive letter-writing campaign deluged state senators and the president himself with pro-horse correspondence. Under this pressure, in December 1971, President Nixon signed into law the new status of the mustangs designating all unbranded or unclaimed wild and free-roaming horses and burros to be "living symbols of the historic and pioneer spirit of the West" that should be "protected from capture, branding, harassment or death." To this end, they were "to be considered, in the area where presently found, as an integral part of the natural system of the public lands."

At first glance, these statements would seem to have solved the problem. But, on close inspection, we discover that the wild horses remain in peril. Several refuges keep alive the spirit of the president's declaration. One was established in 1962, on a portion of Nellis Air Force Base in southwestern Nevada. Unfortunately, the area is in fact a bomb- and missile-testing range. We may imagine how secure these horses must feel, in the midst of a setting that makes the Przewalskis' homeland along the China-Mongolia border seem tame by comparison. A second, the Pryor Mountain Wild Horse Range, is occupied by about 150 horses. Although in a remote mountain area, they remain under scrutiny, lest they in some mysterious way "destroy the range." A third western refuge, the Little Book Cliffs Wild Horse Range, near Grand Junction, Colorado, is a forested area of cedar, juniper and piñon, the home of a mere hundred horses. Established at the end of 1980, it is already threatened by proposed oil and gas explorations. Thus we have, in all of the western United States, a total of three refuges, totalling 495,000 acres — of which 435,000 acres are less than hospitable.

A fourth, somewhat less contentious refuge exists in the eastern states, on Assateague Island, off the Virginia seaboard. Horses have lived there for three centuries, perhaps having swum ashore from the wreckage of a Spanish vessel. Even these ponies have seen their territory drastically reduced, this time by the Federal Fish and Wildlife Service. When high seas flooded their traditional grazing grounds in 1962, almost half their numbers were trapped and drowned. Disease wrought further havoc in 1975, but two years later, forty Nevada mustangs were brought in to rejuvenate the herd. As a result, it now numbers some 170 animals, and appears to be thriving under the care of the fire department in nearby Chinoteague.

In spite of the 1971 federal law establishing the mustangs' status, their future remains unresolved. The Bureau of Land Management can still remove horses declared "excess" in accordance with the principles of good land management. Bills to change their hard-won status as "an integral part of the natural system" are frequently presented to Congress. The mustangs have become a sort of scapegoat, blamed for many problems on the open range.

Every year, the roundups continue. The BLM's current goal is to reduce the total number of horses on all of the country's public lands from the current estimate of 55,000, to 31,000 in 2001. Rounding up 10,000 animals per year only keeps pace with the annual population growth of 18 percent. Those animals considered suitable for private ownership have been made available through the BLM's Adopt-a-Horse program since its inception in 1973. At first, the fee was $25, but in 1981 it leapt to $200. As a result of this and of the indiscriminate rounding up of animals, with no selection process to determine adoptability (many of the animals are too old, lame or sick), there are large numbers of unadopted animals being kept in feed yards until they die. Today, birth control programs are being tested, and more care is being taken in selecting horses for the roundups, in the hope that most, or all, of the animals will find new homes, and that, eventually, the necessity for any roundups will be obviated.

And still the roundups persist. Into the desert, to several locations several times a year, come men and their machines. Planes, helicopters and trucks join in the chase, locating and pinpointing the horses in their hideouts, driving them inexorably toward the traps. Helicopters serve as giant airborne cutting horses, herding the mustangs and turning them back, should they attempt to break off in a new direction. Terrified herds gallop through the dustclouds, twisting and turning in vain efforts to shake off the pursuit.

To no avail. The herds are steered to "wings" that funnel them toward a corral. Here the decoy mare awaits, leading them into the trap. Mounted cowboys ride close behind, ready to follow the mustangs if they seek to retrace their steps in a hopeless bolt for freedom — hopeless, because the cowboys, on fresher mounts, will ride them down, rope them in, and drag them back to captivity.

The cowboys are sympathetic men, and truly avoid inflicting injury. But the horses are exhausted in their flight, confined suddenly in a steel-fenced corral crowded with panicked animals. The mustangs jostle and kick, throwing themselves against the fence or making abortive leaps. In these cramped confines, injuries can and do result.

Although aided now by aircraft and machines, it is still the cowboy who finally shuts the gates, a vivid reminder that the history of the American west is a saga of man and horse. Despite the laws, the publicity campaigns, and the best of intentions, that saga continues, unfortunately to the horse's detriment.

An unusual albino Spanish mustang
mare and foal at the Spanish
Mustang Registry in Oshoto,
Wyoming.

Left: Sunset in Oshoto. Several families gather quietly in the last light of the day.

Above: Classic markings identify this Medicine Hat. The mainly white coat has darker patches on the chest and across the head.

Overleaf: A stallion leads his harem at full gallop across the valley in an early morning ritual.

The nursing mustang foal has faint
fingermarks on its upper forelegs.

While its dam drinks, this foal waits
anxiously nearby.

Left: Well cared-for on the Spanish Mustang Registry, this mare and her leggy foal show no real concern at the approach of the photographer.

Above: A mustang family gathers on a hill after its early morning gallop.

Overleaf: Dusk falls in Oshoto.

The Pryor Mountain Refuge in
Montana, encompassing a variety of
extraordinary landscapes (*above* and
right), is home to some two hundred
mustangs.

Left: High in the Pryor Mountains a mustang grazes quietly.

These three mustangs prick their ears as they sense an intruder.

Timid and suspicious by nature, these Pryor Mountain horses (*above* and *right*) are constantly alert to danger, and able to melt into the background at the first sign of danger.

Overleaf: Led by the dominant mare, a large harem files across a valley floor in the Pryor Mountains.

Against a magnificent backdrop of
forest and rock outcrops, several
Pryor Mountain harems come
together in an extraordinarily large
gathering.

A mare and foal move tranquilly
through the cactus of their home
near Burnt Springs, Nevada.

Left: A lone stallion stands defiantly in the Little Book Cliffs Range in Colorado after his family has fled.

A helicopter pilot drives three Nevada mustangs towards the waiting roundup crew.

As they enter the wing fence that
will funnel them towards the trap,
these four mustangs start to panic,
their escape cut off by the horseman
on the left.

Coats lathered, manes flying, eight mustangs are finally trapped.

Overleaf: A powerful mustang stallion outstrips his pursuer even after being chased some distance earlier by helicopter.

A proud black stallion at the close of day.

POSTSCRIPT

Wherever we may live, our attitudes toward, and our treatment of wild and feral horses serve as a statement of our responses to all of our wildlife, all of our wilderness, and to the larger issues of societies faced with the necessity of conservation. Whether we decide to take positive and effective action to preserve our environments, sharing them with the species that make them their rightful homes, will determine the quality of our lives, and the lives of those who follow us. And if the horse — of all creatures the most closely allied with man throughout the centuries — fails to touch us and motivate us to greater efforts, then today will be infinitely the poorer, and all our tomorrows a bitter might-have-been.

ACKNOWLEDGEMENTS

This book would not have been possible without the help and encouragement of many people. In particular, I wish to thank the following for their involvement:

Photographs:
Sable Island, pages 2, 29, 30, 52–53, 135–141, Zoe Lucas
the Tarpans, pages 70, 75–79, Ralph Crane
the cave art, page 25, M. Norbert Aujoulat
the Brumbies, pages 142, 149, Australian Picture Library, pages 147, 148, © John Carnemolla, Australian Picture Library.

Research:
Carolyn Moulton, Keith Dunnet, Rosemary Phelan and Krista Luik and, for the original idea, Kim McDonald.

Paintings:
pages 18–19, Linda Montgomery.

In France, Dr. Luc Hoffmann, Dr. Patrick Duncan, Claudia Feh and all of the staff at La Tour du Valat and, in Paris, Dr. Vera Eisenmann.

In England, Chris and Gill East, Stuart and Julia Cooper, Mrs. Watts and Derek Sparks; Mrs. Newbolt-Young and the Coaker family; Miss MacNair and Dr. A.W. Gentry. Thanks, too, to Brian and Joyce Harbury.

In the U.S.A., thanks are due to Lloyd Tillet and family, Emmet and Gioja Brislawn, Dr. Oliver Ryder, Bud Brown, Pat Schmidt, Jeff Edwards, Tom Combs, Dawn Lappin, Milt Frei and Jerry Merrick and his roundup crew, Susan West and Hope Ryden.

For their support over a long haul, Ann Bromley, Brant Frayne, Monte Hummel of World Wildlife Fund Canada, Philip Meretsky, Howard Stulberg, Robin Ward and Ed Hailwood.

The assistance of the Ontario Arts Council in the writing of this book is greatly appreciated.